The Prophetic Critique of the Priority of the Cult

The Prophetic Critique of the Priority of the Cult

A Study of Amos 5:21–24 and Isaiah 1:10–17

Theresa V. Lafferty

PICKWICK *Publications* · Eugene, Oregon

THE PROPHETIC CRITIQUE OF THE PRIORITY OF THE CULT
A Study of Amos 5:21–24 and Isaiah 1:10–17

Pickwick Publications
An Imprint of Wipf and Stock Publishers
199 W. 8th Ave., Suite 3
Eugene, OR 97401
www.wipfandstock.com

ISBN 13: 978-1-61097-488-2

Cataloging-in-Publication data:

Lafferty, Theresa V.
    The prophetic critique of the priority of the cult : a study of Amos 5:21–24 and Isaiah 1:10–17.

    XIV + 94 p. ; 23 cm.—Includes bibliographical references and index.

    ISBN 13: 978-1-61097-488-2

    1. Bible. O.T. Prophets—Criticism, interpretation, etc. 2. Bible. O.T. Isaiah—Criticism, interpretation, etc. 3. Bible. O.T. Amos—Criticism, interpretation, etc. 4. Worship—Biblical teaching. I. Title.

BS1515.2 .L22 2012

Manufactured in the USA

This work is dedicated to my parents, Francis J. and Patricia A. Lafferty, who provided me with the foundation of my faith, and for teaching me:

אִם לֹא תַאֲמִינוּ כִּי לֹא תֵאָמֵנוּ

unless your faith is firm you shall not be firm! (Isa 7:9)

This work is also dedicated to my brothers and sisters whose prayerful support has helped to make this work possible.

οὗτοι μόνοι συνεργοὶ εἰς τὴν βασιλείαν τοῦ θεοῦ,
οἵτινες ἐγενήθησάν μοι παρηγορία

these alone are my co-workers for the kingdom of God,
and they have been a comfort to me. (Col 4:11)

This work, finally, is dedicated to my teachers, especially Sister Anne Veronica, IHM, who inspired in me a love for the Word of God and a desire to study it more in depth:

תֵּן לְחָכָם וְיֶחְכַּם־עוֹד הוֹדַע לְצַדִּיק וְיוֹסֶף לֶקַח

give wisdom to the wise man, and he becomes wiser still;
teach the just man and he will add to his learning. (Prov 9:9)

In loving memory of my brother, Gene.

Contents

Preface

THIS BOOK IS A reworking of my doctoral dissertation. I have long been interested in studying the Bible, particularly the Old Testament because it is filled with so many stories and people about whom I knew very little. My interest in the prophets Amos and Isaiah came about because I found their prophecies to and about the people in the northern and southern kingdoms respectively had very little to do with the places where the people worshipped in comparison to what they said about what the people did when they worshipped. Earlier studies introduced me to the Deuteronomists' attitude toward any site for worship other than the Temple in Jerusalem, yet these eighth-century BC prophets did not express the same thoughts. Rather, Amos and Isaiah took issue with the priority given the activities occurring inside the temples over the importance of behaving in a just and right manner in the community outside the temples. I have found that the prophets neither intended to eliminate the cult, nor can their arguments be relegated to mere promotion of social justice in the community. These prophets criticized personal and familial interactions, dealings within the community, and the attitudes with which the people approached Yhwh in the practice of the cult. This book will focus specifically on two oracles in which the cult praxis is called into question, why they are brought to the people's attention in the eighth century BC, as opposed to another time, and what the prophets suggest the people should claim as their first priority.

Acknowledgments

I WISH TO THANK DAVID Bosworth, friend, colleague, mentor, who has helped me wade through the quagmire of post-doctoral defense activities, and most especially for continuously answering the question, where do I go from here?

Abbreviations and Critical Texts Used

AB	Anchor Bible
ABD	David Noel Freedman, editor, *The Anchor Bible Dictionary*
ANET	James B. Pritchard, editor, *Ancient Near Eastern Texts*
AOAT	Alter Orient und Altes Testament
ASOR	American Schools of Oriental Research
BDB	F. Brown, S. R. Driver, and C. A. Briggs, *Hebrew and English Lexicon of the Old Testament*
BHS	*Biblia Hebraica Stuttgartensia*
BibS(N)	Biblische Studien
BTB	*Biblical Theology Bulletin*
BZAW	Beihefte zur ZAW
CAD	*The Assyrian Dictionary of the Oriental Institute of the University of Chicago*
CBA	Catholic Biblical Association
CBQMS	Catholic Biblical Quarterly Monograph Series
FOTL	Forms of the Old Testament Literature
HALOT	W. Baumgartner et al., *Hebrew and Aramaic Lexicon of the Old Testament*
HKAT	Handkommentar zum Alten Testament
HTKAT	Herders theologischer Kommentar zum Alten Testament
ICC	International Critical Commentary

JNSL	*Journal of Northwest Semitic Languages*
JSOT	*Journal for the Study of the Old Testament*
JSOTSup	JSOT Supplement Series
KAT	Kommentar zum Alten Testament
NICOT	New International Commentary on the Old Testament
OTL	Old Testament Library
OTM	Old Testament Message
SBL	Society of Biblical Literature
SBLDS	SBL Dissertation Series
SJLA	Studies in Judaism in Late Antiquity
STDJ	Studies on the Texts of the Desert of Judah
TDOT	G. J. Botterweck et al., editors, *Theological Dictionary of the Old Testament*
VT	*Vetus Testamentum*
VTSup	VT Supplements
WMANT	Wissenschaftliche Monographien zum Alten und Neuen Testament
ZAW	*Zeitschrift für die alttestamentliche Wissenschaft*

For the Hebrew text I use *Biblia Hebraica Stuttgartensia*, edited by K. Elliger and W. Rudolf (Stuttgart: Deutsche Bibelgesellschaft, 1983). The Greek text of Amos is taken from the edition of Joseph Ziegler, *Duodecim prophetae*, Septuaginta: Vetus Testamentum Graecum 13 (Göttingen: Vandendoeck & Ruprecht, 1984). The Greek text of Isaiah is taken from the edition of Joseph Ziegler, *Isaias*, Septuaginta 14 (Göttingen: Vandenhoeck & Ruprecht, 1983). For the Latin translation, I use *Biblia Sacra: Iuxta Vulgatam Versionem*, Robertus Weber, ed., 4th ed. (Stuttgart: Deutsche Bibelgesellschaft, 1994). The text of 1QIsa^a is taken from *The Great Isaiah Scroll (1QIsa^a): A New Edition*, Donald W. Parry and Elisha Qimron, editors (Boston: Brill, 1999). *The Dead Sea Scrolls Bible: The Oldest Known Bible Translated for the First Time into English*, Martin Abegg, Jr., Peter Flint, and Eugene Ulrich, editors (San Francisco: Harper, 1999) 271–72, was also consulted.

All translations are my own, except where noted.

1

The Israelite Cult and
Prophetic Critique

THIS CHAPTER BEGINS WITH a survey of the ancient Israelite cult, its significance, and its critique by the eighth-century BC prophets. Relevant biblical texts that contain a critique of the cult will be assembled and examined in terms of where they occur, what they specifically criticize about the cult, and on what basis the criticism is made. Following this, I will provide a review of previous scholarship on the topic of cult criticism in the OT, with special attention to the prophetic material, especially that of Amos and Isaiah. I will conclude with a summarizing statement concerning the cult-critical texts of the OT on which this book will focus, the reason why they have been selected, and how they will be studied.

INTRODUCTORY REMARKS

The purpose of this book is to clarify prophetic criticism of the cult within the cultural and religious context of the eighth century BC.[1]

---

1. I define the cult as any ritual activity, public or private, associated with homage to a deity. Therefore, it can consist of offerings, sacrifices, prayers, singing, or celebrations of feast days. De Vaux (*Ancient Israel*, 271) defines cult thus: "By 'cult' we mean all those acts by which communities or individuals give outward expression to their religious life, by which they seek and achieve contact with God." Other terms used by scholars to express the same idea include "ritual" (Rowley, *Moses to Qumran*, 67–107; Haran, *Temples*, 205–29); "worship" (Westermann, *Elements*, 187–204); and "sacrifices and offerings"

Ancient Israelites expressed their relationship with Yhwh—among other things—by their participation in the cult and festivals. Sacrifices and offerings were the primary activities at the temples. The preexilic prophets criticized this cultic activity, although they did not suggest that all elements of the cult should be eliminated or abandoned forever.[2] The critique of the cult that the prophets offered was meant to prompt the Israelites to change their focus from external events to internal impulses that would lead them to act rightly towards their neighbors. This study aims to highlight the issues the prophets addressed in relation to the cult. Their criticism of the people's lack of charity, kindness, and care for each other, even as they looked to continue to receive blessings from God, is evident from the statements of these prophets.

Place and Significance of the Cult in Ancient Israel

George Buchanan Gray writes: "Cultic activity is the stuff of which an-cient religions were made. The praxis, the administration of the cultic establishments, the vested interests of the clergy, and the celebrations of the festivals were not mere functions of a systematic religious outlook, devoid of intrinsic importance. They are the index of religion as it was practiced in the life of a society."[3]

A glance through the OT confirms Gray's statement concerning the Israelite cult. The Temple in Jerusalem was built for worship of Yhwh (1 Kgs 5:19) on a grand scale (1 Kgs 5:27–32). The Temple's location on

(Milgrom, *Studies*, 119–21). The prophets Amos and Isaiah criticize particular aspects of the cult, as defined above; therefore I will make no distinction between the cult in the northern and southern kingdoms. While there are specific problems mentioned in the Bible regarding the cult of the northern kingdom, Amos, with the exception of the late addition of 5:26 on which see pp. 27, 41–42 below, does not address those issues in the text with which this book is concerned. Therefore, the term "the cult" will refer to the same legitimate activities that occurred in both kingdoms as defined above.

2. Barton ("Prophets," 113) says that some scholars may argue, "It is simply not con-ceivable that anyone in ancient Israel could have been so radically anti-ritualistic as the texts seem to imply. Religion, it is suggested, was so intimately bound up with sacrifice and ritual that no-one could have opposed them per se without stepping outside the culture altogether." Barton refers to Psalm 50:9–12 and avers, "I cannot see that this can be interpreted other than as a total opposition to the practice of sacrifice in itself" (117). Barton's own argument, however, is inconsistent and fails to clarify the issue of whether or not the intention of the prophets was to eliminate the sacrificial system altogether. On Barton, see my discussion on pp. 10–11.

3. Gray, *Sacrifice*, x.

the top of a hill (2 Chr 3:1), its structure (1 Kings 6) and furnishings (1 Kgs 7:13–51) proclaimed to all the central position the cult held in the life of Israel. Leviticus 1–7 and Numbers 28–29 describe the numerous kinds of sacrifices and offerings, as well as the times of and reasons for the feast days on the Israelite calendar. The lengthy descriptions of the vestments worn by the priests (Exodus 28), and their consecration (Exodus 29; Leviticus 8) demonstrate the importance attached to these persons. There are likewise biblical texts that report the large number of sacrifices offered to Yhwh (1 Kgs 8:5, 62–63; 1 Chr 29:21–22; 2 Chr 29:32–35; 30:24–25; 35:7–9). The existence of cultic practices is not in dispute in the life of ancient Israel. Rather, that such an institution should be portrayed in a negative light by the eighth-century prophets, is what attracts attention.

Biblical Texts that Contain a Critique of the Cult

The following is an inventory of all the texts that contain criticism of the cult, or some aspect of it, in the OT:

a. Amos 4:4–5; 5:21–27
b. Hos 2:13–15; 6:4–6; 8:13; 13:2
c. Isa 1:10–17; 29:13; 43:24; 58:6; 66:3
d. Mic 3:4; 6:6–8
e. Jer 6:19–20; 7:8–10, 17–18, 21–23; 14:12
f. Mal 1:10; 2:13
g. Pss 40:7–8; 50:7–15; 51:18–19
h. 1 Sam 15:22
i. Prov 15:8, 29; 21:3, 27; 28:9
j. Ezek 20:39
k. Zech 7:13
l. Eccl 4:17

The criticism of the cult in these texts may be categorized in five different ways. Excluding the two texts that are the topic of this book, there are thirty passages in the above list that can be categorized as follows: six mention idol worship (Hos 2:13–15; 13:2; Isa 66:3; Jer 7:8–10, 17–18; Ezek 20:39); three passages cite unsolicited offerings (Amos 4:4–5; Jer 6:19–20; 14:12); one accuses the people of performing their sacrifices only out of obedience to the laws (Isa 29:13); six contain a rejection of Israel's cult because of the evil deeds, i.e., the sins, of the people (Isa 43:24; Hos 8:13; Mic 3:4; Zech 7:13; Mal 1:10; 2:3); and fourteen passages state exactly what Yhwh prefers to the worship that is being offered (1 Sam 15:22; Pss 40:7; 50:7–15; 51:18–19; Prov 15:8, 29; 21:3, 27; 28:9; Eccl 4:17; Isa 58:6; Jer 7:21–23; Hos 6:4–6; Mic 6:6–8).

The feature shared by each of the first four categories of texts cited above is the lack of proper attitude and respect for the relationship between the Israelite people and their God. For a people whose God is Yhwh, worship of idols or worship only out of obedience to the law is unacceptable. To come forward with illicit gifts or as a perpetrator of corruption in one's transactions with fellow Israelites likewise does not demonstrate a proper relationship with God. What is above all required by Yhwh, according to many of the fifth group of passages mentioned above, is doing right and justice.[4] The relationship each person had with his fellow Israelites, according to the prophets, should be a reflection of their relationship with Yhwh. Eakin writes: "For the prophets mere legalities were largely unimportant. What was vitally significant was the individual's treatment of his fellowman. Transgression of the neighbor's inherent worth as a creature of Yahweh was anathema, whether the means to the transgression was legal or not. 'Man's inhumanity to man' was more than a social problem for the prophet, nor could he have contented himself with political programs that emphasized man's relationship to his fellow while ignoring his relationship to God."[5]

REVIEW OF PREVIOUS SCHOLARSHIP ON PROPHETIC CRITICISM OF THE CULT

From Wellhausen to Klawans

This section provides a selective review of previous scholarship concerning the topic of criticism of the cult in the OT. I examine the work of representative scholars who have addressed the topic of prophetic criticism of the cult in the past one hundred fifty years.

Any study of scholarship concerning Israel's cult must begin with Julius Wellhausen (1878) who highlights the drastic differences between

4. See also de Vaux, *Ancient Israel*, 454.

5. Eakin, *Religion*, 238–39.

the preexilic and postexilic praxis of the cult. According to him, the influence of the priests, during and after the Exile, on the administration of the cult, whose practice they centralized in the Temple in Jerusalem, and focused specifically on sin and atonement, made the cult less personal than it had been in the preexilic period.[6] The Exile thus became the great dividing line between the joyous personal celebrations of sacrifices in communion with Yhwh and the need for atonement because of the individual and national awareness of sin in the life of the people. Wellhausen examines those portions of the Pentateuch attributed to J/E, the historical books (Judges, 1–2 Samuel, and 1–2 Kings), and the preexilic prophets (Amos, Isaiah, Hosea, Micah, and Jeremiah), in his exploration of the subject of the cult before the Exile. He notes that the stories about sacrifice in the Pentateuch offer insights into the origins of the Israelite cult.[7] He further notes that the only difference between the Israelite cult and that of other ancient cultures was that the Israelites offered gifts to Yhwh, while non-Israelites offered gifts to their gods. In the period of the patriarchs, according to Wellhausen, sacrifice was personal, spontaneous, and joyful. Thanksgiving was the primary purpose of these early sacrifices. The patriarchs, then, were not founders of the cult, but of the holy places to which the people brought their gifts for God.[8] In the historical books, the cult holds a large place in the life of the individual and the community, but the focus is on the sacrifices' being offered to Yhwh alone, rather than to other gods. In fact, according to Wellhausen, aside from the exilic redactional material found in 1–2 Kings, nowhere in the historical books or the preexilic prophetic writings is the cult outside of Jerusalem deemed illegitimate as long as it is offered to Yhwh.[9] In addressing the prophetic criticism of the cult, Wellhausen focuses on the prophets' distinction between the cult and religion. Amos distinguished between worship and faith; according to Wellhausen, Amos's polemic was against the cultic performances of his contemporaries, not against their belief in Yhwh.[10] Wellhausen also asserts the impossibility of Amos's or Isaiah's having recourse to

6. Wellhausen, *Prolegomena*, 53.
7. Ibid., 54.
8. Ibid.
9. Ibid., 55.
10. Ibid., 56.

any written ritual Law because this had not yet been recorded.[11] Thus they had no access to Mosaic instruction or traditions concerning the cult, but only to Yhwh's *tôrâ*, which dealt with matters of justice and morality.[12] In his description of the pre-Law cult in Israel, Wellhausen notes that the "darker sides of pre-Law cult" are known to us from Amos and Hosea; however, he does not explore these texts to determine their deeper meaning, nor does he explain what the "darker sides" of the pre-Law cult are.[13]

The focus of Roland de Vaux's (1958) study concerning sacrifices and the cult is the question: To what extent are the forms of sacrifice mentioned in the J and E redactions of the Pentateuch, in the historical books, and in the preexilic prophets used in Second Temple Israel?[14] He first explains that there are only two kinds of sacrifice in Israel's early period, the עֹלָה, "holocaust" and the זֶבַח, "communion sacrifice."[15] He determines, by examining the relevant biblical texts, that the characteristic feature of the holocaust offering (עֹלָה) was that everything was burnt on an altar.[16] He says that the rubrics of sacrifice were of no concern to the authors of the historical books, although he finds in Gen 22:9–10 and 1 Sam 14:33–34 support for the theory that the victims of sacrifices were usually slaughtered on an altar.[17] De Vaux's discussion further proposes that זֶבַח and שֶׁלֶם are two words for the same sacrifice. The difference between them, according to de Vaux, is that זֶבַח refers to the outward ritual, the way the gift is offered (i.e., it is slaughtered), in contrast to the שֶׁלֶם, which refers to the intention with which the gift is offered (as tribute to God or to maintain or re-establish a good relationship between God and the worshiper).[18] The desert traditions, the Passover, and the Exodus were part of the oral history known to Amos and Jeremiah, according to de Vaux. He says their oracles were not against the cult itself,

11. Ibid., 57.

12. Ibid., 58–61. See also Amos 5:25; Isa 1:10.

13. Ibid., 79.

14. de Vaux, *Ancient Israel*, 426.

15. Ibid., 424. "Holocaust" is the translation of עֹלָה used by J. McHugh in his translation of de Vaux's original French work into English.

16. Ibid., 426–27.

17. Ibid., 427.

18. Ibid.

but rather against the external and material cult since God demands an interior religion that calls for the practice of justice and righteousness, rather than sacrifices on the altar.[19] While both Wellhausen and de Vaux distinguish between the prophetic criticism of the external practice of the cult and the people's own motivations in establishing and maintaining a relationship with God, they do not discuss the consistently anti-cult message of the preexilic prophets. They generalize regarding Israel's cultic praxis based on certain vocabulary items, but fail to discuss those aspects of the cult specifically addressed by the preexilic prophets.

Hans Wilhelm Hertzberg (1962) cites as the basis of the prophets' cult criticism the lack of benefit on the part of God from the merry celebrations of the people on their feast days.[20] Hertzberg operates with a concept of gift giving, or sacrifices, as involving some benefit for the recipient. In this understanding, Israel's festival gatherings were deemed invalid by Yhwh because he does not receive any benefit from them.[21]

Hertzberg proposes, for example, that the problem addressed by Amos is that the celebrations belong to the people, and not to God.[22] For Hertzberg, it was precisely because the temple activity is devoid of any divine participation that the prophets speak against it. Amos's repetition of the term "your" in 5:21–23 ("your feasts," "your solemn assemblies," "your grain offerings," "your fatted animals," "your noisy songs," and "your lyres") emphasizes the prophet's interpretation of the people's actions in the religious realm.[23] Hertzberg says that, rather than offering sacrifices, the prophets declared that the people should do the will of God, behave rightly, and that this would lead to a direct relationship with God.[24] Hertzberg notes that the prophets observed the discrepancy between life and the cult, and that their job, in the service of God, was to speak out against abuses of the cult since the practice of the cult should have represented the moral life of the people.[25]

19. Ibid., 428; see also Amos 5:25; Jer 7:22.
20. Hertzberg, *Traditionsgeschichte*, 83.
21. Ibid.
22. Ibid.
23. Ibid., 81.
24. Ibid., 83.
25. Ibid., 82.

Hans Boecker (1981) looks particularly at preexilic prophetic criticism of the cult.[26] He recognizes that the prophets' cult criticism employs a distinctive language and that the prophets were charged with teaching the Israelites that religion is a process that developed over time.[27] Such teaching reflects the prophets' ability to initiate a change in the concept of religion from a magic-ritual stage to an ethical-moral stage.[28] According to Boecker, the prophets uncompromisingly rejected the cult because of their conviction that ritual actions could no longer repair the relationship of the people with God.[29] The prophets discouraged the praxis of the cult because it could no longer effect its intended purpose. The prophets claimed that the practice of the cult had become senseless and perverted.[30] Therefore, the prophets make clear that the cult is only being performed for the sake of Israel's own interests, irrespective of how God receives it.[31] This situation explains why Amos 5:21 refers to "your feasts" and "your assemblies" and Isa 1:11 exhibits the same pronominal usage, "*your* sacrifices." Boecker then investigates whether the common message and language of the prophets who criticize the cult can be explained by the literary dependence of Isaiah on Amos, and rejects such dependence.[32] Boecker also discusses H. Gunkel's claim of an influence of the psalms on the prophets' words, but denies any such correlation because the prophets criticize music and prayers in addition to animal sacrifice, while the psalms do not.[33] Finally, Boecker looks to wisdom traditions, which direct attention to ritual actions and usually use antithetical parallelism to articulate their instructional message, as potential source material available to the prophets when they composed their criticism of the cult.[34] He notes that wisdom traditions teach that the internal attitude of the one who offers is reflected in the kind of

---

26. Boecker, "Überlegungen zur Kultpolemik," 169–80.

27. Ibid., 172.

28. Ibid.

29. Ibid., 174.

30. Ibid., 175.

31. Ibid., 176.

32. Ibid.

33. Ibid., 178.

34. Ibid.

ritual act performed.[35] If a person rejects the instruction of the law, then his prayer, which is his ritual action, is considered repugnant (Prov 28:9).[36] The prophets refer to the cult that Israel performs as the cult of the wicked, which is an atrocity to Yhwh that can only be rejected.[37] While Boecker concludes that prophetic cult criticism is not identical with Wisdom cult criticism, he notes that its starting point might be sought and found here.

Alexander Ernst (1994) studies and compares the texts of Amos 5:21–27 and Isa 1:10–17 in order to determine the origins of their criticism of the cult.[38] He compares the language used in these texts to that of the Priestly texts, and determines that there are similarities.[39] However, Ernst states that these similarities only demonstrate the prophets' knowledge of Priestly traditions; such similarities do not indicate that the prophets were priests.[40] The first person verbs in the text of Amos 5:21–23 are indicative of prophetic speech as opposed to the language typical of priests.[41] The prophets' total rejection of the cult, without differentiation between those sacrifices offered by good or wicked people, contradicts what the priests would teach as the basic condition of the cult: that Yhwh is ritually attainable.[42] Ernst considers the wisdom traditions as the closest parallel to the language of Amos 5:24 given its call to right behavior, use of the word pair "justice and righteousness," and of comparison.[43] Where Amos deviates from wisdom traditions, though, is in an absolute announcement of punishment (5:27).[44] Ernst understands the threat to all Israel, in the form of exile, as stemming from the prophet's foreknowledge which led to his insight into the futility of the cult.[45] Holding that priestly and wisdom traditions may be linked to the prophetic oracles, Ernst attempts to

35. Ibid., 179.
36. Ibid.
37. Ibid., 180.
38. Ernst, *Kultkritik*, 97–178.
39. Ibid., 162.
40. Ibid., 114.
41. Ibid., 115.
42. Ibid.
43. Ibid., 121.
44. Ibid., 122.
45. Ibid., 118.

answer the question: what function does ethical language play in light of the prophets' rejection of ritual?[46] He establishes that their background knowledge of wisdom's ethics and of the cult enabled Amos and Isaiah to voice what Yhwh desires most of all as a matter of the people's behavior. These prophets' criticism of the cult do not judge the cultic actions, or the goodness of the gifts offered, or the piety with which the prayers are offered. Instead, the prophets instruct the people that they must perform appropriate merciful behavior toward one another. Such behavior determines whether God accepts the cult, or declares it an atrocity.[47] Thus, Amos's and Isaiah's familiarity with priestly language and wisdom traditions influences how they phrase their messages, but the essence of their message is uniquely prophetic.

Walter Brueggemann (1997) rejects the conception of OT theology deriving from classical Protestantism with its profound aversion to cult and finding value only in the OT's prophetic-ethical traditions.[48] He affirms that scholars should take a careful look at the practice of worship in Israel, because worship is where Israel worked out its unique identity and sustained its distinctive life in the world.[49] He further points out that the cult did become a place of self-indulgence and satiation and that Yhwh became a function of a religious enterprise that was manipulative and self-satisfying.[50] Brueggemann maintains that the prophets were concerned with gross abuses in the cult and would not have entertained the notion of abolishing the cult; rather, they taught the cult should be a witness to and embodiment of the practice of communion with Yhwh.[51] So he concludes that the cult is a place wherein Israel could be in the presence of God, and there is no evidence that the prophets opposed public worship itself, so long as the worship focused on Yhwh.[52]

Barton (2005) compares the anti-cult statements attributed to pre-exilic prophets with the pro-cult statements of postexilic prophets.[53] He

46. Ibid., 161.
47. Ibid., 172.
48. Brueggemann, *Theology*, 651.
49. Ibid., 653.
50. Ibid., 678.
51. Ibid.
52. Ibid.
53. Barton, "Prophets," 113.

identifies a consistent opposition to the cult prior to the exile on the basis of Amos 4:4–5; 5:21–22; Hos 6:6; Mic 6:6–8; Isa 1:11–13; and Jer 7:22, declaring these passages "*prima facie* evidence of prophetic opposition to the cult."[54] Barton goes on to affirm that it is inconceivable that the prophets in ancient Israel could have such radically negative attitudes against the cult as the texts imply.[55] Rather, he argues, religion was so bound up with the cult that anyone who was opposed to the practice of the cult *in toto* would have to have separated himself from Israelite culture.[56] As Barton proceeds, he addresses the argument of scholars who deny the viability of the rituals in ancient Israel and who promote the idea of religion as consisting of "right social interaction."[57] A problem with Barton's argument is that he never explains the postexilic prophetic statements in favor of the cult, which far outnumber the statements against the cult from preexilic prophets. If the preexilic prophets were anti-cult and preferred right actions, and they were correct in so doing, then how can the postexilic promotion of the cult be explained?

Jonathan Klawans (2006) presents a thorough analysis of the modern study of prophetic cult criticism and concludes that the opposition of the prophets to sacrifice reflects the social and economic messages of the prophets themselves.[58] He argues that in their criticism of cultic activity the prophets expressed their opposition to sacrifices and offerings, although they never intended to deny the validity of cultic worship *per se*. He suggests that the gifts presented for sacrifice were rejected because the offerings themselves, the material gifts presented, had been stolen from their original owners.[59] "The concern with property renders it impossible to sharply distinguish between a ritual violation and an ethical wrong. Sacrificing a stolen animal is, at one and the same time, both ethically and ritually wrong."[60] Klawans's argument is based on his reading of prophetic statements concerning sacrifices in conjunction with "expressions of concern over the economic exploitation of the

---

54. Ibid., 111–12.
55. Ibid., 113.
56. Ibid.
57. Ibid., 116–21.
58. Klawans, *Purity*, 75–100.
59. Ibid., 98.
60. Ibid.

poor" as found in Amos 5:10–11 taken together with Amos 5:23, or Isa 1:11–15 read in light of Isa 1:17.[61] In so depicting the members of the Israelite society as "thieves," the prophets, according to Klawans, accuse all in the society as being guilty of, or at the very least liable for, crimes within their community.[62] That the priests would (albeit unknowingly) accept stolen goods for ritual purposes implies that they assumed legitimate ownership on the part of the one bringing the gift.[63]

Klawans's argument wanders off course when he declares that cult criticism and the OT purity laws must be joined together as a single issue for study. His work on biblical sacrifice is based on the Priestly material in Leviticus, which formalizes and ritualizes every act of sacrifice. Klawans affirms that purity and sacrifice were not separated Temple spheres or functions.[64] Such a claim makes clear that his argument derives from a postexilic perspective. None of the prophets of the eighth century shows any concern for the topic of purity per se, except, possibly, Isaiah in 1:16a: "Wash up! Clean up!"[65] While he does briefly discuss the prophetic critique of sacrifice, Klawans groups all such criticism together, such that he analyzes all four eighth-century prophets along with Jeremiah (seventh century) and Ezekiel (early exilic), Samuel and Elijah (prophetic characters found in the books of Samuel and Kings), as well as the criticism found in Psalm 40 and Proverbs (wisdom literature). To his credit, Klawans understands the problem of rejection of sacrifices as a matter of prioritization.[66] But to combine so many different writings together and analyze them as constituting one single group, is to deny the connection every prophet had with a specific time period (such as the eighth century). Klawans's procedure fails to attend to the impact that each prophet's criticism of the practice of the cult would have had on his own original audience.

In summary, there is much scholarly precedent for studying pre-exilic prophetic criticism of the cult. The scholars cited above recognize prophetic rejection of sacrifice as a signal to the people that Yhwh does

---

61. Ibid., 87.

62. Ibid., 88.

63. Ibid.

64. Ibid., 48.

65. Isaiah 1:16 will be discussed in chap. 4.

66. Klawans, *Purity*, 81.

not appreciate something they are doing. The earliest scholarship denied the importance of the cult based on the prophets' criticism of it.
Recent scholarship explains the prophets' criticism as an effort by the
prophets to redirect attention to the concept of social justice. Although
debate has lasted over 100 years, the question of the status of preexilic
cult practice according to the prophets has not yet been definitively answered. Scholars have yet to fully explain the phenomenon of criticism
of the cult in preexilic Israel.

Synthesis and Evaluation

As illustrated in the above section, scholars have approached the topic
of the cult from many angles. Wellhausen avers that sacrifice was only
practiced in Israel because the neighboring culture, i.e., the Canaanites,
performed sacrifices to their gods. Thus, Wellhausen claims, Israelite
sacrifice is not of Mosaic origin. However, Israelite sacrifices were being
officially offered in the Temple in Jerusalem for at least two centuries by
the time Isaiah decried the practice. Why would a two hundred year old
practice suddenly be declared unacceptable?

A different argument is from de Vaux who says that the cult was an
appropriate practice, but that offerings would only be acceptable if the
people also practiced righteousness and justice. Hertzberg disagrees, as-
serting that God has no need of the cult and that the cult was rejected
because of abuses in its praxis. Hertzberg asserts that the celebrations,
especially of feast days, were of the people, for the people, and by the
people. God had no place, no role, no part. God underscores the problem in his repetition of "your" when describing the feasts, solemn assemblies, grain offerings, fatted animals, noisy songs, and lyres in Amos
5:21–23. While Hertzberg thus explains that it was God's noninvolve-
ment that rendered the cult unacceptable, he does not explain how this
situation came to be so one-sided.

Boecker focuses on the word pair מִשְׁפָּט and צְדָקָה, "justice" and
"righteousness," as a way of explaining the prophetic call to practice
social justice. He says that the OT laws serve as a basis for justice, beginning on a family level and expanding up to the entire Israelite society.
The problem with this argument is that it focuses only on the problem
of social justice, and fails to address the problem of the validity of the
cult for the prophets.

Ernst explores the resources available to the prophets, namely priestly language and wisdom traditions, when they composed their messages. The similarity of the language of the prophets' criticism of the cult to that of some Psalms and wisdom literature and Ernst's denial of the influence of Mosaic traditions on Amos's text, suggests that there is more to the prophets' criticism of the cult than has yet been determined.[67] That Amos and Isaiah were familiar with the temple cult and with wisdom traditions cannot be denied. Ernst rightly concludes that these sources influenced the prophets to criticize the roles that people played in their lives inside and outside the sphere of the cult. The question he leaves unanswered is to what extent the prophets utilized the above sources and yet were able to maintain the prophetic character of their messages.

Brueggemann identifies the practice of the cult as a witness, or as testimony, that one is behaving in a just manner. Like de Vaux, Brueggemann claims that the prophets argued that the people needed to have the priority of righteousness and justice brought to their attention prior to their bringing gifts to the Temple. A problem with this thesis is that the treatment of others with justice and righteousness can be understood to have been a prerequisite of Israelite behavior at least from the time of the Sinai Covenant. Seventy percent of the Decalogue deals with just and right treatment of others. The criticism of the cult is a consistent message of the eighth-century prophets. Neither de Vaux nor Brueggemann provides an explanation for the sudden appearance on the scene of messengers from God who criticize common practice in the Temple.

Barton lists five preexilic passages that oppose the cult and proceeds to examine the argument that religion in Israel could exist without the practice of the cult. Moral reform in Israelite society, as a means to be forgiven for one's sins, is preferred by Yhwh to the practice of the cult. Therefore, the insult to Yhwh is only compounded if offerings are brought by sinful people. A problem with this argument is that some sacrifices, some cultic behaviors, were meant specifically to remove the burden of sin that people bore who did not behave properly in the society. Such a circular argument does not resolve the issue of the validity, or lack thereof, of the cult.

67. Ernst, *Kultkritik*, 105.

Klawans mentions the economic impact of the change from a primarily subsistence economy to one based on class as the reason that
God rejects the people's offerings. He offers no reason, however, as to
why the prophets of the eighth century would suddenly decry temple
cult practices. The whole society was assuredly not responsible for il-
legal real estate transactions or illicit weights and measures in the mar-
ketplace. However, the cult as a whole, including recitation of prayers
and the singing of psalms, was rejected by the prophets. Scholars have
simply not yet answered the question of what happened in the eighth
century that Yhwh should suddenly send two messengers with a similar
and shocking message about his rejection of the cult being offered at
two different temples.

There is thus no scholarly consensus about why the cult, which
had been practiced for over two centuries under the tutelage of the
Israelite and Judahite kings, drew the attention of Amos (5:21–24) and
Isaiah (1:10–17), who preached against it. Scholarship has pinpointed
the many economic and social factors operative within Israel and Judah
when these two prophets appeared, but has yet to make the connection
between those factors and the praxis of the cult. Did the cult reflect
the change in economic and social situation of the community? Was
there a sudden change in the activities at the temples that mirrored the
problems in the society? Did the temple priests turn a blind eye to the
plight of the less fortunate in the society, or did they simply not notice
the plight because the underprivileged were absent from the temples?
Whether the cult took place in a northern (Bethel) or the southern
(Jerusalem) temple was of no concern to the eighth-century prophets,
while by contrast the fact of a northern temple being used for Yhwh
worship would become a problematic theme highlighted throughout
the books of Kings. Scholars have yet to address the fact that the messages proclaimed in two different temples are similar, thus making the
critique span the whole of the Israelite community, whether in the north
or the south. The lack of geographic boundaries for the message may be
a key to understanding it. Scholars have suggested that Amos 5:21–24
may have been a source for Isaiah's oracle (1:10–17), but there has been
no discussion to date about whether Amos composed his oracle based

on the message of another prior source.[68] I plan to address these issues in this book in order to elucidate the meaning of the two oracles.

AMOS 5:21–24 AND ISAIAH 1:10–17

Of the texts inventoried above, the two on which I will focus are Amos 5:21–24 and Isa 1:10–17, given the remarkable similarity of the two passages.[69] Also, the missions of the two prophets occurred at about the same time in the eighth century BC. The book of Amos (1:1) reports that Uzziah ruled in the south, while Jeroboam II reigned in the north.[70] The book of Isaiah (1:1) only provides the names of the rulers in the southern kingdom, in the period from Uzziah through Hezekiah.[71] As will be shown in more detail in chapters three and four, Amos 5:21–24 and Isa 1:10–17 both present approximately the same message. Each purports to be a direct quotation from Yhwh (Amos 5:16–17; Isa 1:10–11). Each passage negates similar aspects of the cult (Amos 5:21–23; Isa 1:11–15).[72] Each prophet delivers his message in a temple: Amos goes

---

68. Fey (*Amos und Jesaja*) investigates the connection between the two prophets, Amos and Isaiah, and concludes that Isaiah used Amos as a primary source. Ernst (*Kultkritik*, 163–69) succinctly states that two possibilities present themselves regarding the similarities of the two texts: either the text of Isaiah depends on that of Amos, or both prophets rely on a common older source (ibid., 163). Ernst says that while Isaiah knew of the Amos text, Isaiah should not be viewed as a simple "conglomerate of Amos reminiscences" (ibid., 164). Rather, *contra* Fey, Ernst says that Isaiah shows no literary dependence on Amos, and in fact, lacks the certainty of imminent disaster that Amos predicts for all Israel in 7:8 and 8:2 (ibid., 165). Ernst thinks that Isaiah quite possibly assumes the function of a priest in 1:10, even though the words he uses there reflect a wisdom influence (ibid., 169). The text that follows in vv. 11–17 is inconceivable coming from a priest, but finds a parallel in the wisdom material, so that, for Ernst, there is a possibility that Isaiah is dependent upon, not Amos, but wisdom tradition.

69. Ernst, *Kultkritik*, 161.

70. Amos 1:1; Uzziah reigned for 52 years (2 Chr 26:3); the consensus among scholars is that he died around 742 BC. Jeroboam II reigned 786–746 BC. This narrows Amos's preaching to sometime between 786 and 746 BC.

71. The dates of the four kings named in Isa 1:1 range from 794 to 687 BC. Isa 6:1 states that the prophet's call came in the year Uzziah died (ca. 742) and he continued until about 701 BC. Isaiah prophesied in Jerusalem (Isaiah 6).

72. Ernst (*Kultkritik*, 114) avers that the texts criticize various aspects of the cult, including prayer and music. He further states that the vocabulary used by the two prophets in these particular passages has in view the whole of the cult and the variety of its possibilities and intentions (ibid., 116).

to the northern temple in Bethel (7:10–13), and Isaiah cries out in the Temple in Jerusalem.[73] The similarity in form and content of the two passages calls for further inquiry into the reason for and meaning of their composition.

METHODOLOGY

I conclude this chapter by laying out the methodology I will follow in the remaining chapters. Chapter two will outline the background for study of Amos 5:21–24 and Isa 1:10–17. The social, economic, and religious situation of Israel and Judah will be explored on the basis of the relevant biblical and extra-biblical sources and a general orientation to the books, persons, times, and overall messages of the two prophets, Amos and Isaiah, will be provided. Chapters three and four focus on the exegesis of the two texts selected for study. These texts will be examined using the following outline:

1. Delimitation of the Text— in which I discuss the limits of the particular text under discussion.
2. Text and Translation—in which I offer the Hebrew text with my translation.
3. Literary Form—in which I will discuss the linguistic structure, genre, and life setting of the text.
4. Structure of the Text—in which I discuss the unity of the text.
5. Authenticity and Dating—in which I consider arguments bearing on the authenticity and dating of the unit.
6. The Unit in its Context—in which I attempt to determine the relationship between the text and its proximate and wider contexts in the book as a whole.
7. Exegetical Analysis—in which I look at each verse individually.
8. Conclusion—in which I provide a summary of my findings on the given text.

73. Wildberger, *Isaiah 1–12*, 38–39.

Finally, I will end in chapter five with a comparison of the two passages, a short discussion of the differences observed therein, and my conclusions.

2

The Social, Economic, and Religious Situation of the Eighth Century

INTRODUCTION

I N THIS CHAPTER I will begin with a description of Israelite society in the eighth century BC. By that point, the monarchy had been established and functioning for two centuries in Israel. In addition to the many independent self-sufficient rural farms of the Israelites, villages had grown to accommodate the needs of the king and the staff who were in his employ.[1] In this chapter I will also present a general orienta-

---

1. Borowski (*Daily Life*, 13) states, "The growth of the village trend . . . is attributed to the relative stability and tranquility provided by the Israelite monarchies. Others think that the expanding number of villages in the [Iron Age] IA II was the outcome of the changing character of the cities during this urban phase. They were gradually filled up by nonresidential structures, which forced most of their inhabitants to leave. The cities became occupied predominantly by members of the state administration. Thus the bulk of the population moved out of the cities into the countryside to live in villages and farmsteads." De Geus (*Towns*, 161) notes that the average settlement size was between four and eight hectares, or ± ten to twenty acres, and so such a settlement should be referred to as a town. He notes that the capital of Israel, Samaria, because of its size, was the only true city at this time. However, the words "city" and "cities" are used in the Bible and by modern scholars when referring to the settlement wherein the king resides, even if in terms of its size this settlement was no larger than a town.

tion to the books attributed to Amos and Isaiah, and will review what can be known of these two men and their overall messages.

Among Israel's neighbors, Assyria was on the rise as a national threat. Egypt and Babylonia were quiet for the time being. The Canaanites, who continued to live among the Israelites, played a role in the development of Israelite political, social, and religious structures.[2]

During this period of relative calm, prophets arose in Israel and Judah who drew attention to the negative aspects of society and its religious practices, with Amos prophesying in Israel and Isaiah in Judah. I will now turn to an examination of the state of affairs within Israel and Judah during the eighth century.

INTERNAL SITUATION OF EIGHTH-CENTURY ISRAEL AND JUDAH

The Temple in Jerusalem, according to the biblical text, was built by Solomon in the tenth century BC and was well established as a national shrine for Yhwh by the eighth century. There were also other shrines, some extant from before the erection of the Temple in Jerusalem, in use at Bethel, Dan, Shechem, and Gilgal, in the northern kingdom.[3] By the eighth century the kingdom was already split into two smaller units: Israel in the north and Judah in the south. Urban areas arose which housed primarily the employees of the king, while those who farmed or kept livestock moved further away from the cities.[4] Market areas developed where merchants provided goods to the city-dwellers such as cloth, pottery, food, and other necessary supplies.[5]

The majority of the population lived outside of the cities, in the land better suited for raising crops and pasturing animals.[6] Storehouses

---

2. King and Stager, *Life*, 352; Smith, *Early History*, 19; Borowski, *Daily Life*, 7. For an opposing view regarding Canaanite influence on the Israelites, see Roberts, "Defense," 377–96.

3. For these sites, see: Bethel: Amos 3:14; 4:4; 5:5; 7:10–13; Dan: Amos 8:14; Shechem: Hosea 6:9; and Gilgal: Amos 4:4; 5:5; Hosea 4:15; 9:15; and 12:11.

4. Borowski, *Daily Life*, 13.

5. Ibid., 56.

6. Borowski (ibid., 13) points out, "In the IA–II (ca. 1000–sixth century BCE) most of the population (66 percent) resided in small villages and the rest in settlements (towns, cities) larger than twelve acres."

were built to keep the harvests for future use. As time progressed and farmers became more adept at the processes of agriculture, they were able to utilize their surplus stores for trade.[7]

In the eighth century problems began to surface with regard to the new social and economic structures of Israelite society. The elders at the city gates were tempted to judge in favor of their friends and family, thus leaving the poor, widows, and orphans without anyone to advocate their cause (Amos 5:12; Isa 1:23; Mic 3:11; 7:3).[8] Merchants, whose livelihood depended on the buying and selling of goods, might keep two sets of shekel-weights, the heavier set for buying, and the lighter for selling (Amos 8:5; Hos 12:8).[9] Families that formerly depended upon every member's effort for survival began to lose members to the military draft or conscription for the king's building projects.[10] Sometimes, the work that called the men away from home (military campaigns, major building projects) resulted in their loss of life. Their widows and orphans who were thus left to fend for themselves did not always receive fair treatment at the markets or in judicial matters.[11] Thus, eighth-century Israel was growing and changing politically, economically, and socially, but not in an altogether positive way, according to the prophets who voiced their criticisms of these developments.

Another aspect that is difficult to quantify, but should at least be acknowledged, is the presence in Israel of influences from other cultures, particularly that of the Canaanites, whom the Bible lists among the pre-Israelite residents of the land (Gen 15:19–21; Exod 3:8). Walter Kornfeld argues that the Israelite monarchy was established on the basis of a known and established Canaanite model, such as found at Tyre and Sidon.[12] Although Kornfeld further states that in OT texts prior to the Babylonian Exile that speak of "Canaanites," the word "Canaanite" is synonymous with "trader," I do not agree that the two terms are identical in every case.[13] Such stereotyping of an entire people can cause

---

7. Ibid., 26.
8. Ibid., 53–54; Albertz, *History*, 1:161; Houston, "Social Crisis," 141.
9. Weinfeld, *Social Justice*, 9; Premnath, *Prophets*, 95–96.
10. Albertz, *History*, 1:159–63.
11. Weinfeld, *Social Justice*, 36–37.
12. Kornfeld, "Gesellschafts," 181–200.
13. Ibid., 185. See Isa 23:8; Hos 12:8; Zeph 1:11; Job 40:30; Prov 31:24 for cases in

many problems and does not help in understanding the people and the culture in the land when the Israelites arrived. Kornfeld also avers that fraudulent business practices, such as false measures and weights, were standard and "quite legitimate" operating procedures for the Canaanites, yet, he cites no evidence for this statement.[14] According to Kornfeld, since the Canaanites had already created a social system wherein wealthy officials restricted the rights of the lower classes, when the Israelite kings annexed formerly Canaanite areas, the Canaanite administrative and economic systems were also adopted by the new Israelite kingdom—a claim that is refuted in current scholarship.[15] I do not deny that the Canaanites had some influence on the economy, government, and social systems in the Israelite kingdom(s), but I do not think such influence was as great as Kornfeld advocates.

Regarding the material and ritual of Israelite sacrifice, Smith provides an extensive comparison of Ugaritic sacrificial terms with their counterparts in biblical Hebrew.[16] It is likewise Kellermann's contention that the Israelites learned and replicated the עֹלָה from the Canaanites, although the Israelite practice of whole-burnt offerings probably preexisted Israelite interaction with the Canaanites.[17] Judges 6:25–26 and 1 Kings 18 support Kellermann's argument, as does 2 Kgs 10:1–28, when Jehu appears to follow Canaanite ritual practices as a ruse to identify all the worshipers of Baal (v. 19).[18] Thus, it is difficult to ascertain the extent of Canaanite influence on the Israelites within the religious realm. While the Israelites did establish their own recognizable political and social spheres, the continuing Canaanite influence upon them in the secular realm, to a greater or lesser extent, cannot be denied.

---

which Canaanite and trader may be used synonymously. However, there are sixty-five biblical references to Canaanites where "trader" would not be an appropriate rendering. See, for example, Gen 10:18; Exod 23:23; Num 13:29; Deut 11:30; Josh 5:1; Judg 1:1; 2 Sam 24:7.

14. Kornfeld, "Gesellschafts," 185.

15. Ibid., 184. Such refutation may be found, for example, in Roberts, "Defense," 380.

16. Smith, *History*, 22–24.

17. D. Kellermann, "עוֹלָה/עֹלָה," 11. 109.

18. Ibid.

EXTERNAL SITUATION OF ISRAEL AND JUDAH: ASSYRIA

In this section I call attention to Assyria as the key external factor in the life of late eighth-century Israel. There are a number of biblical and extrabiblical references to the situation in the eighth century BC, and, in particular, to the interactions between the Assyrians and the Israelites.

Assyria lay northeast of Israel and posed the most significant threat to Israel during the late eighth century. Although it is never mentioned by Amos, Assyria became a serious threat as the eighth century wound down. The kings of Assyria in the second half of the eighth century expanded and strengthened their kingdom. Tiglath-Pileser III (744–727 BC) founded and greatly expanded the Assyrian empire.[19] According to the biblical record, he threatened Pekah, the king of Israel in Samaria (2 Kgs 15:29), and received tribute from Ahaz, the king of Judah (2 Kgs 16:7–19; 2 Chr 28:20). Isaiah attempted to intervene in the Judean crisis by appealing to Ahaz to remain faithful to Yhwh.[20] Sargon II (722–705 BC) is noted for his capture of Samaria, which turned Israel (Northern Kingdom) into an Assyrian province (2 Kgs 18:9).[21] Again, at the end of the century, during Sennacherib's campaign against Jerusalem following the death of Sargon II, Isaiah provided advice to King Hezekiah in Judah (701; Isaiah 36–37).[22] The presence of Assyria as a serious threat to Israel and Judah was a constant background for the messages of the eighth-century prophets. Isaiah and Micah prophesy that Yhwh is going to use Assyria as a punitive means to correct the problems within Israel and Judah.[23]

GENERAL ORIENTATION TO AMOS

As indicated previously, the two eighth-century prophets of primary interest for this book are Amos and Isaiah. Each prophet's book is dated

19. Roberts, "Egypt," 268. See also Hoffmeier, "Egypt's Role," 285–89.

20. Blenkinsopp, *Isaiah 1–39*, 100.

21. Roberts ("Egypt," 270) and Younger ("Assyrian Involvement," 237–38) date the fall of Samaria to 720 BC.

22. Ussishkin, "Campaign," 339–57; Younger, "Assyrian Involvement," 245–50; Blenkinsopp, *Isaiah 1–39*, 100.

23. Isa 11:16; 27:12; Mic 5:4–5; 7:12.

with reference to the reigning kings in the mid to late eighth century BC.[24] Amos 1:1 also alludes to an earthquake.[25]

The Book and its Formation History

The book of Amos is the third book of the Twelve Minor Prophets in the MT, falling between Joel and Obadiah. This book is the earliest written collection of prophetic oracles preserved as an independent work.[26]

The book of Amos is primarily composed of poetry (chaps. 1–6) together with narrative visions and an epilogue (chaps. 7–9). It may be outlined as follows:[27]

I. Poetry

    A. Chapters 1–2

        1. Oracles against nations (1:3—2:3)

        2. Oracles against Israel and Judah (2:4–8)

    B. Chapters 3–6

        1. Oracles and riddles (3:1–8)

        2. Messages for Israel and Samaria (3:9—4:3)

        3. Messages for all Israel (4:4–13)

        4. Lamentation over Israel (5:1–17)

        5. Coming Day of Yhwh (5:18–20)

        6. Criticism of Israelite cult (5:21–27)

        7. Woes and warnings (6:1–14)[28]

II. Narrative Visions and Epilogue: Chapters 7–9

    A. Five visions (7:1–3, 4–6, 7–9; 8:1–2; 9:1–4)

    B. Amaziah confronts Amos (7:10–17)

24. See chapter 1, nn. 70–71.

25. Yadin (*Hazor*, 150–51) excavated Stratum VI (eighth century BC) at Hazor and identified a level likely destroyed by an earthquake, given that the building walls at that level were atilt and the ceiling pieces scattered on the floors showed signs of having been knocked abruptly from their supports.

26. Paul, *Amos*, 1.

27. The following commentaries were consulted for the above outline of Amos: Wolff, *Joel and Amos*, viii–ix; Andersen and Freedman, *Amos*, x–xiii; Paul, *Amos*, vii–viii.

28. Andersen and Freedman (*Amos*, xxxv–xxxvi) identify seven woes in the following verses: 6:1aα; 6:1aβ; 6:3a; 6:4a; 6:4b; 6:5a; and 6:6a.

C. Oracles concerning the end (8:4–14)

D. Epilogue (9:7–15)

Amos employs a wide variety of literary genres in his work, including judgment speeches (4:1–3); dirges (5:1–17); exhortations (3:1–12,
13–15; 4:1–5; 5:1–7, 10–17; 8:4–6); vision reports (7:1–8; 8:1–2; 9:1–4);
narratives (7–9); and eschatological promises (5:18–20; 8:9–10, 13–14;
9:11–12).[29] He also utilizes metaphors and similes (2:9; 3:12; 5:2, 7, 19,
24; 6:12; 9:9); paronomasia (5:5b; 6:1, 7; 8:2); irony (5:20; 6:12; 9:4, 7);
and sarcasm (3:12, 4:4–5; 6:1).[30] Amos confronts his audience with their
own words (2:12; 4:1; 5:14b; 6:13; 7:16; 8:5, 14; 9:10) and asks didactic
questions (2:11; 3:3–6, 8; 5:18, 25; 6:12; 8:8).[31] The number five figures
prominently in Amos's material: he lists five examples of God's actions
on behalf of Israel in its early history (2:9–11); he repeats the negative
particle לֹא five times in 2:14–16; the refrain וְלֹא־שַׁבְתֶּם עָדַי נְאֻם־יְהוָה, "and
you did not return to me, declares Yhwh" appears five times in 4:6–11;
five cosmic acts of God are cited in the doxologies of 4:13 and 5:8; five
vision reports occur in chaps. 7–9; and five curses are spoken against
Amaziah in 7:17.[32] Finally, Amos expresses completeness with uses of
the number seven (or seven plus one): seven oracles against foreign nations in 1:3–2:5 climax with an eighth against Israel; seven rhetorical
questions culminate in an eighth referring to prophecy in 3:3–8; and
seven units of the Israelite army will be unable to escape according to
2:14–16.[33] Amos betrays familiarity with wisdom traditions by his use
of graded numerical oracles in chaps 1–2.[34] Although wisdom sayings
were usually meant to instruct, Amos employs such sayings to intro-
duce God's consistent message of judgment against each of the countries named in these chapters.[35]

Chapters 3–6 show that Amos directed his oracles toward the
people of Israel, citing several vivid examples of their behavior that

29. Paul, *Amos*, 4–5; Andersen and Freedman, *Amos*, 12.
30. Paul, *Amos*, 5.
31. Ibid.
32. Ibid.
33. Ibid.
34. Wolff, *Joel and Amos*, 95.
35. Ibid.

required change. Amos observed the effect the accumulation of wealth had on people as manifested in their large building projects and lavish furnishings (3:15; 5:11; 6:4–6).[36] He likewise noted the penetration of such opulence into temple ceremonies and a lavish cult with elaborate rites (4:4–5; 5:21–23).[37]

The book ends with Amos's visions about the future of the people if the Israelites do not heed his word. The first two visions (7:1–3, 4–6) are connected by their allusion to plagues that were already mentioned in 4:6–11. According to the visions, these plagues would afflict both Israel and Judah.[38] The first vision concerns a locust plague (7:1–3), which recalls the locusts mentioned in 4:9.[39] The second vision depicts the destruction of Israel by cosmic fire (7:4–6) and is a parallel to the description of the destruction of Sodom and Gomorrah by fire cited in 4:11.[40] Amos received Yhwh's clarification concerning the meaning of the plagues in his visions; the visions reveal an all-encompassing judgment not previously experienced by Israel: the end of the nation.[41] The problems in Israel were greater than could be rectified by a replacement of a dynasty or by improving the quality of the cult.[42] According to Amos, national repentance was not a matter of formulas and sacrifices, but a change of heart, will and action.[43]

Interspersed among and following the vision reports, chaps. 7–9 include other kinds of material. First is the biographical account, in 7:10–17, in which Amos is dismissed from the temple at Bethel by the priest, Amaziah.[44] There are various oracles (8:4–14) that expand the meaning of the fourth vision (8:1–3).[45] A second series of oracles

---

36. Paul, *Amos*, 2.
37. Ibid.
38. Andersen and Freedman, *Amos*, 83.
39. Ibid.
40. Ibid. In Amos 7:4–6 Amos intercedes for the people and Yhwh relents.
41. Ibid.
42. Ibid., 84.
43. Ibid.
44. Ibid., 763; Paul, *Amos*, 238.
45. Wolff, *Joel and Amos*, 324.

(9:7–10) follows that develop the fifth vision (9:1–6).[46] Finally, there is a late redactional conclusion in 9:11–15.[47]

The identification of authentic and original material attributed to the eighth-century prophet, Amos, has been a point of contention among scholars. Acknowledging that the task is difficult at best, scholars have, nonetheless, attempted to assign particular oracles and passages to various redactors. Wolff, for example, focuses attention on the core material found in chaps. 3–6 that is introduced as either the "words of Amos" (3:3–8; 4:4–5; 5:7, 10–11, 18–20; 6:12); or are introduced by Amos followed by an oracle of Yhwh (3:1a, 2, 9–11, 13–15; 4:1–3; 5:1–3, 12, 16–17; 6:1–7, 13–14); or, finally, are simply presented as oracles of Yhwh (without any introduction by the prophet) (3:12; 5:4–5, 21–24, 27; and possibly 6:8).[48] To these three categories of oracles, Wolff claims, redactors have added, at various times, the rest of the material now found in the book of Amos.[49] Andersen and Freedman address the problem of identifying authentic passages by listing commonly agreed upon redactional elements: 1:2; 1:9–10; 1:11–12; 2:4–5; 2:10; 3:7; 3:14b; 4:13; 5:8–9; 5:13; 5:14–15; 5:26–27; 6:2; 8:6; 8:8; 8:11–12; 8:13; 9:5–6; 9:8–15.[50] I agree with their conclusion, except that no one, at this time, can prove whether or not Amos wrote any particular passage in the book that bears his name. Paul, for example, goes beyond the evidence in claiming that "the book in its entirety (with one or two minor exceptions) can be reclaimed for its rightful author, the prophet, Amos."[51] It is difficult to believe that a book that was composed twenty-eight centuries ago has been transmitted virtually without change. Jeremias claims that the book was edited over a period of three centuries, and that its present form is from the late postexilic period.[52] Moreover, Jeremias claims that the book was first composed after the fall of Jerusalem and

---

46. Ibid.

47. Ibid., 352.

48. Wolff, *Joel and Amos*, 107.

49. Ibid., 107–13. Wolff identifies a total of six periods during which material was composed and edited into the original core message of the prophet Amos.

50. Andersen and Freedman, *Amos*, 142.

51. Paul, *Amos*, 6.

52. Jeremias, *Amos*, 5.

after the book of Hosea.[53] His limited examination of the book's composition and redaction, identifying chaps. 3–6 as an older work, framed by the oracles of chaps. 1–2 and the visions of chaps. 7–9, provides the period following the fall of Samaria as a date for its earliest written form.[54] While Jeremias' arguments for indentifying three distinct units in the book are sound, and no doubt redaction was still occurring in the postexilic period, his late dating of its earliest written material cannot be accepted because it permits no authentic passages to be attributed to the original prophet. In regard to chaps. 3–6, Andersen and Freedman identify nearly the same material as authentic that Wolff did before them and for this reason, I agree with the arguments for authenticity presented by these authors.

Person and Date of Ministry

Amos, whose name means "burden," came from Tekoa, which is located about eight miles south of Jerusalem; however, he prophesied in the temple at Bethel (1:1 and 4:4). He raised sheep and was a dresser of sycamore trees, but not a member of any prophetic guild (7:14). As a shepherd and farmer, Amos was interested in the natural and unnatural seasonal and weather conditions in his country. His imagery was influenced by his profession and acquaintance with nature (2:13; 3:4–5, 8, 12; 4:1; 5:11, 17, 19; 6:12; 7:1–2, 4, 14; 8:1; 9:9).[55] Amos was familiar with some traditions of Israel, such as those concerning Sodom and Gomorah (4:11); the plagues in Egypt (4:10); the Exodus (2:10; 3:1; 9:7); the forty years in the desert (5:25); the conquest of the land (2:9); and David's musical activity (6:5).[56] His book also demonstrates his knowledge of psalmic doxologies (4:13; 5:8–9; 9:5–6) and wisdom traditions.[57] He called for national repentance lest Israel fall prey to the impending plagues.[58]

---

53. Ibid., 5–6.

54. Ibid., 5–9.

55. Paul, *Amos*, 5.

56. Ibid., 4.

57. Wolff, *Joel and Amos*, 91; Paul, *Amos*, 4.

58. Andersen and Freedman (*Amos*, 85) conclude: "Neither plagues nor prophet had any effect on the people or the leaders, north or south. That claim is repeated five times in 4:6–11."

Amos appeared in Israel during the reign of Jeroboam II (787–746 BC) and proclaimed death by the sword for the king (7:11).[59] Israel was experiencing a period of economic prosperity after military successes early in Jeroboam's reign.[60] Thus, commerce flourished (8:5a), trade on an international scale increased (3:9), deceitful business practices generated profits for some (8:5a), costly edifices were being built (3:15), and viniculture and cattle raising were geared toward the needs of demanding customers (5:11b; 6:4b). The economic upswing had an effect on the cult as well. Amos observed sacrificial offerings being increased (4:4–5; 5:21–22), and feasts celebrated with singing and instrumental music (5:23). The economic success of some members of society was gained at the expense of other, less fortunate members. Slavery for debt (2:6; 8:6), exploitation of the poor (2:7a; 4:1; 8:4), and intimidation of witnesses and taking of bribes (2:7aβ; 5:10, 12) became commonplace.[61] The incidents of unfairness recorded by Amos serve to focus attention on the treatment of some people in Israelite society by their fellow citizens during a specific period of economic prosperity in Israel's history.

Overall Message

Three major foci can be identified throughout the book of Amos. First, Yhwh himself is the book's primary focus. Five times Amos claims that Yhwh spoke to him (3:8; 7:1–8, 15; 8:1–2; 9:1–4). Additionally, Amos claims to be passing on Yhwh's message when he begins an oracle with כֹּה אָמַר יְהוָה, "thus says Yhwh" (1:3, 6, 9, 11, 13; 2:1, 4, 6; 3:12; 5:4, 16; 7:17), or ends an oracle with אָמַר יְהוָה, "says Yhwh" (1:5, 15; 2:3; 5:17, 27; 9:15). Amos also identifies certain oracles as נְאֻם־יְהוָה, "utterance of Yhwh" (2:11, 16; 3:10, 15; 4:3, 6, 8, 9, 10, 11; 6:8, 14; 9:7, 8, 12, 13), or נְאֻם אֲדֹנָי יְהוִה, "utterance of ʾăḏōnāi Yhwh" (3:13; 4:5; 8:3, 9, 11). The message that Amos received from Yhwh and passed on had to do with judgment. The people of foreign nations and the Israelites themselves, that is all people, are liable to punishment that will come from Yhwh himself (1:4–5, 7–8, 14; 2:2–3, 23; 3:2, 15; 5:17, 27; 6:8, 14; 7:8; 9:1–4). Amos's announcements of punishment warn that Yhwh will act, usually

---

59. Wolff, *Joel and Amos*, 89.

60. Paul, *Amos*, 1.

61. Wolff, *Joel and Amos*, 90; Andersen and Freedman, *Amos*, 20.

using first person speech attributed to Yhwh.[62] Yhwh is the sole God, responsible also for foreign nations (1:3–8, 13–15; 2:1–3; 3:2; 9:7), and there is no polemic against the cult of foreign gods, with the only exception being the late addition of 5:26.[63] God will use various agents to accomplish his purpose, i.e., foreign nations.[64]

The book's second major topic is Israel. Yhwh is responding and will continue to respond to the Israelites' failure to do justice and righteousness (5:7, 24; 6:12). Israel was chosen from among all the nations (3:2), but its injustice and lack of righteousness are viewed by Amos as a failure by the Israelites to learn from Yhwh's salvific actions and election in the past.[65] Thus, Israel's present and future situation of privilege as the people of Yhwh is in danger because of the people's contempt for the rights of the weak (8:2).[66] The thrice repeated word pair "justice and righteousness" serves to make clear that whereas just and righteous conduct should be having the same effect as life-giving water (5:24), the people have turned justice into poison (6:12) and have forcibly thrown righteousness to the ground (5:7).[67]

The third focus in the book of Amos is the nations. The book begins with oracles against six foreign nations (1:2–2:3), but foreign nations are also mentioned in oracles addressed to Israel (2:9; 3:2; 9:7).[68] Sometimes, the nations are referred to as instruments of Yhwh's punishment, although no specific country's name is mentioned in connection with the impending threat (3:11; 5:3; 6:14; 9:4).[69] Amos was specific, though, in naming the punishment: deportation and exile (4:2–3; 5:27; 6:7; 7:17).[70] The affirmation that Yhwh is the God of Israel and of all

---

62. Wolff, *Joel and Amos*, 102; Andersen and Freedman, *Amos*, 89; Paul, *Amos*, 3.

63. Wolff, *Joel and Amos*, 101.

64. Andersen and Freedman, *Amos*, 91; Paul, *Amos*, 3.

65. Wolff, *Joel and Amos*, 105; Jensen, *Ethical Dimensions*, 90.

66. Wolff, *Joel and Amos*, 103, 106.

67. Ibid., 103.

68. The foreign nations cited are Damascus (1:3); Gaza (1:6); Tyre (1:9); Edom (1:11); Ammon (1:13; 2:9); Moab (2:1); and Egypt (3:2; 9:7).

69. Ibid., 105; Paul, *Amos*, 3.

70. Paul, *Amos*, 3.

the nations is a new element in the message of Amos.[71] The origin and future of all peoples are determined by Yhwh.[72]

GENERAL ORIENTATION TO ISAIAH

Book

The book of Isaiah is the first of the Major Prophets, standing immediately after the books of Kings and followed by the book of Jeremiah, in the MT. At least Amos and Hosea probably had completed their work before Isaiah's ministry began.[73] The book is named for a historical person named Isaiah who was responsible for the origin of the book and whose influence can be recognized throughout its final form.[74] However, the extant book of Isaiah has been understood as the work of at least three different authors, known as First, Second, and Third Isaiah, since the commentary of Bernhard Duhm.[75]

Formation History of Isaiah 1–39

Although it now constitutes a single work, the book of Isaiah was composed over the course of four centuries.[76] Sweeney provides the following timeline for the four major stages of the book's composition and redaction: (1) various texts of chaps. 1–32 that stem from the eighth-century Isaiah, son of Amoz; (2) a late seventh-century edition written to support King Josiah's program of national and religious reform that includes portions of chaps. 5–23; 27–32; 36–37; (3) a late sixth-century edition of the book which incorporates further material into chaps. 2–32; 35–55; 60–62 and was assembled in conjunction with the return of the exiles from Babylon to Jerusalem and the rebuilding of the Temple; and (4) the final form (chaps. 1–66) that was produced in

---

71. Wolff, *Joel and Amos*, 106.

72. Ibid.

73. Wildberger, *Isaiah 28–39*, 495.

74. Ibid., 494. The name Isaiah means "salvation of Yhwh."

75. Duhm, *Jesaja*. Duhm divided the book of Isaiah into three complexes. First Isaiah, chaps. 1–39, is attributed to the original prophet, Second Isaiah, chaps. 40–55, to an exilic author, and Third Isaiah, chaps. 56–66, to a postexilic author who may also have composed portions of the material found in the previous 55 chapters.

76. Sweeney, *Isaiah*, 41; Wildberger, *Isaiah 28–39*, 529; Childs, *Isaiah*, 7.

connection with the reforms of Ezra and Nehemiah in the mid- to late fifth century.[77] Sweeney further notes that each redaction employed earlier material, but expanded this with its own supplementations in an ongoing process that eventually produced the present form of the text.[78]

First Isaiah reflects an eighth-century historical setting.[79] Isaiah prophesied at different periods between the death of King Uzziah (ca. 740; 6:1) and 701, when Sennacherib left Jerusalem (37:37).[80] These periods of ministry were interrupted by longer periods during which the prophet appears to have said nothing.[81] Two major periods of ministry are evident: the time before the Syro-Ephraimitic War and the time after this war.[82] Prior to the war, Isaiah's messages addressed social and community issues; after the war he focused primarily on political events.[83] Isaiah's prophecies can be grouped into four distinguishable periods: (1) during Aram and Israel's threat to Jerusalem (733); (2) when the Northern Kingdom fell to the Assyrians (722); (3) at the time of the Ashdod revolt (ca. 711); and (4) in connection with Hezekiah's revolt against Sennacherib (701).[84] The messages that Isaiah preached during these periods correlate closely with the historical events that were occurring.[85] Yet, it remains difficult to establish the individual redactional phases through which the material passed.[86]

Authentic material attributable to Isaiah is scattered unevenly throughout the first thirty-nine chapters, but can most confidently be identified in chaps. 1–12; 13–23; and 28–35.[87] The majority view regards

77. Sweeney, *Isaiah*, 51. Sweeney's timeline is not widely accepted by scholars; however, I agree with his assertion that the entire book was composed over a long period of time, that is, four centuries.

78. Ibid.

79. Sweeney, *Isaiah*, 41; Wildberger (*Isaiah 28–39*, 513–59) provides an exhaustive history of scholarship concerning the study of Isaiah in which he reviews the various attempts by scholars to resolve questions surrounding the development of chaps. 1–39.

80. Wildberger, *Isaiah 28–39*, 569; Blenkinsopp, *Isaiah 1–39*, 98–101.

81. Wildberger, *Isaiah 28–39*, 562.

82. Ibid., 569.

83. Ibid.

84. Ibid.

85. Ibid.

86. Ibid., 530.

87. Ibid., 534–35. Wildberger explains that authentic material is rather sporadic in

these three blocks of material as distinct collections, each attributed to First Isaiah. Wildberger identifies two expansive complexes of Isaiah's prophecies, each of which is structured chronologically. First, there are authentic passages in the material now found in 2:6–11:9, which contains prophecies of Isaiah from the beginning of his ministry to beyond the Syro-Ephraimitic War as well as prophecies from 717–711.[88] Second, there are messages that likely originated at the time of Hezekiah's revolt against Sennacherib (705–701) now found in chaps. 28–31.[89]

Scholars agree that there were distinct precipitating events that prompted the composition of various blocks of material in First Isaiah.[90] For example, Isaiah entered the public arena in 735 to persuade King Ahaz of Judah to remain calm after the Syrian-Israelite attack (Isa 7:1) and the threat by advancing Assyrian forces (735) under the leadership of Tiglath-Pileser III (744–727). Isaiah's narrative call, a description of the Assyrian threat, and Isaiah's subsequent message to Ahaz are found respectively in 6:1–13; 7:1–17; and 8:1–22.[91] Isaiah emerged a second time during the revolt (714–711) of the Philistine city, Ashdod, against Sargon II (722–705). On this occasion, according to 20:1–6, Isaiah paraded around Jerusalem naked to simulate the fate of prisoners of war.[92] Finally, Isaiah made a third appearance during Sennacherib's (704–681) campaign against Hezekiah in 701. The details of this event are described in chaps. 36–37.[93] The accounts of each of these events that are recorded in the book of Isaiah seem to have been written in close proximity to the happenings they describe, but not necessarily by Isaiah himself.[94] Such

---

Isaiah 13–23; in 24–27, the prophet does not speak at all; in 28–35, the "authentic" passages are mainly found in 28–31.

88. Ibid., 541.

89. Ibid.

90. Sweeney, *Isaiah*, 59; Blenkinsopp, *Isaiah 1–39*, 91; Wildberger, *Isaiah 28–39*, 534–38.

91. Sweeney, *Isaiah*, 59; Blenkinsopp, *Isaiah 1–39*, 91; Wildberger, *Isaiah 28–39*, 535–36.

92. Blenkinsopp, *Isaiah 1–39*, 91.

93. Ibid., 91; Wildberger, *Isaiah 28–39*, 537.

94. Blenkinsopp, *Isaiah 1–39*, 91; Wildberger, *Isaiah 28–39*, 535. Although scholars vary widely concerning the scope of what was written by the eighth-century prophet, they generally agree that at least the passages cited above were recorded during the periods listed. For example, Sweeney (*Isaiah*, 59) and Wildberger (*Isaiah 28–39*, 535–42) assign much more material to the eighth-century prophet than does Blenkinsopp.

broader questions about the composition history of Isaiah 1–39 are not, however, directly relevant here since there is general agreement that the passage Isa 1:10–17 is from Isaiah himself. In any case, First Isaiah ends with chap. 39.[95] It is on the segment Isaiah 1–39 that I shall now focus in the outline below.[96]

Outline of Isaiah 1–39

I. Chapters 1–12

A. Introductory Chapter (1:1–31)

1. Superscription (1:1)

2. Prologue to the book—introductory announcement of Yhwh's intention to purify Jerusalem (1:2–31)

B. Oracles against Judah and Jerusalem (2:1—12:6)

1. Second superscription (2:1)

2. Vision of future peace (2:2–5); parallels Mic 4:1–5

3. Oracles concerning judgment on Jerusalem (2:6–4:6)

4. Restoration of Davidic rule (5:1—12:6)

a. Isaiah's memoir (6:1—8:18)

b. Announcement of a new ruler (9:1–7)

II. Chapters 13–27

A. Oracles against foreign nations (13:1—23:18)

B. The "little apocalypse" (24:1—27:29)

III. Chapters 28–39

A. Series of woes (28:1–4; 29:1–4, 15–16; 30:1–5; 31:1–3; 33:1)

1. Oracles concerning Yhwh's plans for Jerusalem (28:1—31:9)

2. Description of just and peaceful government, deliverance from foes (32:1—33:24)

95. Wildberger, *Isaiah 28–39*, 498.

96. The following commentaries were consulted for my outline of Isaiah 1–39: Kaiser, *Isaiah 1–12*, v–vi; Jensen, *Isaiah, 7–10*; Wildberger, *Isaiah 1–12*, v–vi; Wildberger., *Isaiah 13–27*, v–vi; idem., *Isaiah 28–39*, v–vi; Sweeney, *Isaiah, 39–40*; Brueggemann, *Isaiah*, v–viii; Blenkinsopp, *Isaiah 1–39*, vii–x; Childs, *Isaiah*, vii–ix. No two of these commentaries provide exactly the same outline.

B. Contrast between the evil empire and the restored City of
God (34:1—35:10)

.1. Judgment on Edom (34:1–17)

2. A promise of salvation (35:1–10)

C. Episodes that report Isaiah's interaction with King
Hezekiah (36:1—39:8 // 2 Kgs 18:13—20:19)

1. Crisis when Sennacherib invaded Judah
(36:1—37:38)

2. Isaiah announces healing for Hezekiah (38:1–22)

3. Prediction of the Babylonian Exile (39:1–8)

Like Amos, Isaiah employs numerous literary genres, many utilizing parallelism, the basic characteristic of Hebrew verse.[97] Genres used by him include a dirge (1:21); psalms (12:1–6; 25:1–5; 33:2–6; 38:9); oracles (13:1; 15:1; 17:1; 19:1; 21:1, 11, 13; 22:1; 23:1); woe sayings (1:4, 24; 5:8, 11, 18, 20, 21, 22; 10:1, 5; 16:4; 17:12; 18:1; 28:1; 29:1, 15; 30:1; 31:1; 33:1); a proverb (14:4–21); and symbolic action accounts (7:3; 8:3; 20:1–6). There are also recurring motifs, such as light and darkness (5:20; 8:22; 9:1), vision and blindness (6:10; 29:9, 18; 32:3; 35:5), and judgment by fire (1:7; 4:4–5; 26:11; 29:5–6; 30:27, 30; 31:9).[98] Examples of Isaiah's use of literary sound patterns include paronomasia, anaphora, and onomatopoeia (1:2, 4; 3:1; 5:7; 7:9; 24:16, 17).[99] He also uses many titles for Yhwh, such as יְהוָה צְבָאוֹת "Yhwh of Hosts" (more than seventy times in First Isaiah); אֱלֹהֵי יִשְׂרָאֵל "God of Israel" (17:6; 21:10, 17; 24:15; 29:23; 37:16; 21); קְדוֹשׁ יִשְׂרָאֵל, "Holy One of Israel" (1:4, 24; 5:19, 24; 6:3; 10:20; 12:6); אֲבִיר יִשְׂרָאֵל "Strong One of Israel" (1:24); אֱלֹהֵי יַעֲקֹב "God of Jacob" (2:3); אֵל גִּבּוֹר "Mighty God" (10:21); אֱל־בֵּית יַעֲקֹב "God of the House of Jacob" (29:22); and קְדוֹשׁ יַעֲקֹב "Holy One of Jacob" (29:23).

Person and Date of Ministry

Little is known of the personal life of Isaiah. He was the son of Amoz (1:1) and received a personal call from Yhwh in the Temple in Jerusalem (6:1–13). To all appearances, his prophetic work was done in Jerusalem

97. Blenkinsopp, *Isaiah 1–39*, 79.
98. Ibid., 80.
99. Ibid., 80–81.

of Judah in the eighth century.[100] His message was, at times, directed also against Israel (9:7, 8, 20; 17:3; 28:1, 3) and Samaria (9:8; 10:9; 17:3).[101] Apart from Jerusalem, not a single other city of Judah is ever mentioned in Isaiah 1–39.[102] When Jerusalem and Judah are mentioned together, the capital city is always named first (3:8; 5:3).[103] Isaiah is quite familiar with Jerusalem and its surrounding regions. He mentions the waters of Shiloh (8:5); the Valley of Rephaim (17:5); the House of the Forest and the Lower Pool (22:11); and Mt. Perazim (28:21).[104] His familiarity with these places suggests that Isaiah was a citizen of Jerusalem.[105] He was apparently married to a "prophetess" (8:3) who bore him two sons who were given names symbolic of his message to the people (7:3; 8:3).[106] His access to Kings Ahaz (7:3) and Hezekiah (37:1–7) indicates that he may have been from the aristocratic class, while his knowledge of wisdom traditions points to his being an educated person.[107]

Overall Message

As was the case in the book of Amos, Isaiah's book features major topics that run throughout the work. These topics become evident already through the repetition of key words or phrases. For example, Isaiah refers to God in a number of ways to demonstrate his belief that Yhwh is not simply the God of Jerusalem and Judah, but of all Israel (northern and southern kingdoms).[108] Isaiah also presents images of Yhwh as a father (1:2–3), teacher (2:3), vinedresser (5:1–7), king (chap. 6), barber (7:20), farmer (28:24–28), judge, lawgiver and king (33:22). In all his various roles, Yhwh should, but often does not, receive the respect due him from his people.

100. Sweeney, *Isaiah*, 51.

101. Wildberger, *Isaiah 28–39*, 560.

102. Ibid. Sodom and Gomorah are mentioned in 1:9, 10, but only as sites long ago destroyed.

103. Wildberger, *Isaiah 28–39*, 560.

104. Ibid., 561.

105. Ibid.

106. Isaiah's two sons' names are שְׁאָר יָשׁוּב, "A remnant shall return" (7:3), and מַהֵר שָׁלָל חָשׁ בַּז, "Swift booty, speedy prey" (8:3).

107. Jensen, *Isaiah*, 20.

108. Wildberger, *Isaiah 28–39*, 561.

If Isaiah thinks of and refers to God via exalted titles, he also gives much attention to the relationship between God and the people. On eleven occasions the Judahites are called עַמִּי, "my people" (1:3; 3:12 [*bis*], 15; 5:13; 10:2; 19:25; 22:4; 26:20; 32:13, 18). This usage stands in contrast to the nine times where God speaks disparagingly of הָעָם הַזֶּה, "this people" (6:10; 8:6, 11, 12; 9:15; 28:11, 14; 29:13, 14). On four occasions, the Israelites are called God's בָּנִים, "children" (1:2, 4; 30:1, 9), this indicating a still more intimate relationship than the phrase "my people."

Isaiah also highlights the idea that a remnant will survive the impending trouble and will be converted. The reference to a remnant that will return is repeated eight times in First Isaiah (1:9; 10: 20, 21, 22; 16:14; 28:5; 37:4, 32), where the fate of the remnant of Israel is compared with the remnant of Babylon that will be destroyed (14:22, 30).

In analyzing the overall message of First Isaiah, one must look at its major topics and determine how they all fit together. The God of the Israelites, יְהוָה צְבָאוֹת, is also God of the foreign nations and capable of using them to carry out his punishments on Israel. Yhwh considers the Israelites not simply his own people, but also at times his children. Though punishment is inflicted on those children, a remnant will be saved and will carry on the relationship that God has with Israel.

The similarities of Isaiah's message to that of Amos highlight the problems of injustice in eighth-century Israel and Judah. Isaiah's use of the key concept of justice (1:21), as well as his concern for the underprivileged (1:23), his criticism of leaders who do not lead (3:12), his condemnation of those who abuse the poor (3:15), his disapproval of inequitable judgments (10:2), and his denunciation of deep-seated dishonesty (29:15), is reminiscent of the messages of other prophets of the same time period. Like Amos, Isaiah criticizes the Temple cult (1:10–17). Amos's censure of the people's false worship (Amos 4:5) is echoed in Isaiah's similar statement (Isa 29:13). Both prophets denounce the ruling elite and their wives (Isa 3:16–4:1; Amos 4:1–3). The two prophets defend the rights of the poor, widows, orphans, and disenfranchised members of society (Isa 5:8–13; Amos 6:1–7). Finally, each identifies certain specific offenses, e.g., judicial corruption and acceptance of bribes (Isa 1:23; 5:23; 10:1–2; 33:15; Amos 2:7–8; 5:10).

CONCLUSION

The priority given to cultic worship by their audiences is one of the problems addressed by Amos and Isaiah. For those audiences, the principal means of communication with God were the activities that took place in the temples. The prophets perceived that such temple activities had become their hearers' only forms of worship, and that once the people left the confines of the place of worship, they behaved in ways that were incongruent with their status as people who claimed Yhwh as their God. The internalization of their relationship with Yhwh that should have been strengthened by their temple participation was being neglected. The blessings they sought were withheld by Yhwh because their outward behaviors did not express any sort of concern for others.[109] A closer look at two prophetic pericopes that address such problems with the cult of respectively, Israel and Judah, will follow in the next two chapters.

---

109. Brettler ("Nevi'im," 458) states, "A close reading of prophets such as Isaiah or Amos suggests that they are not anti-law or anti-Temple, but are rhetorically emphasizing that ritual behavior alone, without proper moral behavior, is insufficient to assure divine blessing."

3

Amos 5:21–24

INTRODUCTION

ISRAELITE WORSHIP OF THE eighth century BC, as defined above in chapter one, involved the offerings and sacrifices made in a temple, prayers and psalms sung in a temple, and celebration of Sabbath and festival days.[1] Amos is the first among the eighth-century biblical prophets to decry temple worship and to suggest a different way of revering Yhwh.[2]

In this chapter I will discuss Amos 5:21–24. I will examine the text as it appears in *BHS*.[3] The pericope will receive a verse-by-verse exegesis, with consideration given to the various methods of criticism mentioned in my first chapter. The chapter will conclude with a brief summary.

---

1. A distinction is made here between the Temple in Jerusalem and all other temples. Only the building located in that city will be referred to with a capital letter; all rival sanctuaries (Bethel, Dan; see 1 Kgs 12:29–31) will be referred to in lower case.

2. Amos prophesied in the temple in Bethel in the Northern Kingdom, Israel (Amos 7:10).

3. No fragments of the text of 5:21–24 have been identified among the finds at Qumran.

DELIMITATION OF THE TEXT

The book of Amos may be divided into three composite sections, based on the genres found within those sections.[4] Following the superscription and title in 1:1–2, the first section consists of chaps. 1–2 and contains oracles against foreign nations and also against Judah and Israel.[5] The prophet's final oracle in this section (2:6–16), which is against Israel, is an introduction to the heart of Amos's message to Israel, which follows in chaps. 3–6.[6] The middle section, chaps. 3–6, includes the bulk of Amos's message to the people of Israel, and is punctuated by repetition of the formulas שִׁמְעוּ אֶת־הַדָּבָר הַזֶּה, "hear this word" (3:1; 4:1; 5:1), and הוֹי, "woe" (5:18; 6:1).[7] The final section (chaps. 7–9) is primarily a record of Amos's visions, although it also incorporates some biographical material (7:10–17) and an epilogue (9:7–15).[8]

In chap. 5, Amos instructs Israel to "seek" Yhwh (v. 4), but not in any of the sanctuaries (v. 5). The prophet lists some matters about which Yhwh takes offence, such as crooked judgments and denying justice (v. 7), lying (v. 10), cheating and abusing the poor (v. 11), and accepting bribes (v. 12). There follows an exhortation to repent and to establish justice (vv. 14–15), and a call for public lamentation over the people's behavior (vv. 16–17). In vv. 18–20 Amos announces the coming Day of Yhwh, a day on which the impending punishment will befall the people.

4. For more on the basic three-part structure of the book of Amos, see King, *Amos*, 21; Auld, *Amos*, 50; Jeremias, *Amos*, 6, 12; and Wolff, *Joel and Amos*, 107. Different divisions are proposed by Andersen and Freedman (*Amos*, 16), who divide the book into three books: the Book of Doom (chaps. 1–4), the Book of Woes (chaps. 5–6), and the Book of Visions (7:1—9:6), plus an Epilogue (9:7–15); Mays (*Amos*, 12) distinguishes between the sayings spoken by the prophet, the first-person narratives told by the prophet, and the third-person narratives reported about the prophet. Watts (*Vision and Prophecy*, 1–2) divides the material into a book of "words" in chaps. 1–6, autobiographical visions in 7:1–9; 8:1–3; and 9:1–6, and the biographical narrative in 7:10–17, while Paul (*Amos*, 6–7) identifies six bodies of material that can be grouped according to their common literary genre: oracles against foreign nations, oracles introduced by the phrase, "Hear this word," woe oracles, visions, biographical narrative, and independent oracles grouped together because of their common theme of judgment.

5. Andersen and Freedman, *Amos*, 12; Wolff, *Joel and Amos*, 107; Paul, *Amos*, 6.

6. Andersen and Freedman, *Amos*, 323, 325; Paul, *Amos*, 6–7.

7. Jeremias, *Amos*, 48, 83; Paul, *Amos*, 100–101; Wolff, *Joel and Amos*, 92–94. See the discussion in Andersen and Freedman, *Amos*, 461–63.

8. Wolff, *Joel and Amos*, 294; Paul, *Amos*, 222–4; and Andersen and Freedman, *Amos*, 611.

The form of these verses, the "woe-cry," is recognizable, given the use of הוֹי plus the plural participle.[9] Chapter 6 begins with another הוֹי plus plural participle construction (הוֹי הַשַּׁאֲנַנִּים בְּצִיּוֹן, "Woe to those in Zion who are complacent") which signals a change of scene and a new pericope.[10]

This chapter focuses on the text of 5:21–27, which falls between the two woe-cries of 5:18–20 and 6:1–7.[11] The change in style from direct address of the prophet to the people in vv. 18–20 to first person divine speech in vv. 21–27 indicates the start of a distinct unit.[12] Similarly, the introduction of a new unit is signaled by the occurrence of הוֹי, "woe," at the start of 6:1.

THE UNITY OF 5:21–27

The divine speech of vv. 21–27 is distinguished by the poetic form of vv. 21, 22aβ–24, 27 and the prose of vv. 22aα, 25–26.[13] Such a stylistic change indicates the hand of a redactor and militates against the inclusion of the prose verses as part of the original unit.[14] Additionally, the common theme of exile in vv. 26–27 links the two verses.[15] Wolff and Jeremias read v. 27 as part of the original oracle because the announcement of punishment is attached to the preceding material, just as occurred in

9. Wolff, *Joel and Amos*, 254. Wolff discusses the rhetorical form "woe-cry" on pp. 242–45.

10. Ibid., 273.

11. Ibid., 260, 273; Paul, *Amos*, 188, 199; Jeremias, *Amos*, 109.

12. Wolff, *Joel and Amos*, 260; Andersen and Freedman, *Amos*, 523; Paul, *Amos*, 188; Jeremias, *Amos*, 101; Mays, *Amos*, 106.

13. Andersen and Freedman, *Amos*, 530; Wolff, *Joel and Amos*, 262. Verse 22aα interrupts the bi-cola structure of the rest of the oracle and contains a protasis without a matching apodosis (Mays, *Amos*, 106). Another problem with v. 22aα, according to Wolff (p. 259), is that it breaks the pattern already begun in v. 21 of subjects with pronominal suffixes, given its change of subject and the absence of a pronominal suffix with עֹלֹת.

14. Loretz, "Gottesnamen," 288; Mays, *Amos*, 106, 112–13; Wolff, *Joel and Amos*, 258–60; Jeremias, *Amos*, 103–6; and Andersen and Freedman, *Amos*, 537 (v. 27b only). For opposing arguments, see Andersen and Freedman, *Amos*, 530–7, who insist on the unity of vv. 21–27; Paul, *Amos*, 190, 193–98. Paul (p. 197) unconvincingly argues for second-hand influence of a Mesopotamian astral cult during the period of Amos's prophecy, and rejects taking v. 26 as an addition of a later hand.

15. Paul, *Amos*, 194; Jeremias, *Amos*, 105; Andersen and Freedman, *Amos*, 543; Mays, *Amos*, 110, 113.

the oracles against the foreign nations in 1:3—2:16.[16] However, the topic of vv. 26–27 is a prophecy concerning what is going to happen in the future. The complete change of subject from that of vv. 21–24 indicates vv. 26–27 are also a later addition to the unit.

The use of מִנְחָה "grain offering" in vv. 22aα and 25, although the former uses the plural form and the latter the singular, marks both verses as additions of a later redactor because it is not until the Deuteronomist that the biblical texts use separate terms for animal offerings and grain offerings to signify the scope of cultic offerings.[17] Verse 22aα, כִּי אִם־תַּעֲלוּ־לִי עֹלוֹת וּמִנְחֹתֵיכֶם, "even if you offer up to me whole-burnt offerings" functions as a concession that reflects "the interest of a later glossator"; in particular, because the phrase העלה עלות, "the offering up of whole-burnt offerings," is common in the Chronicler's history.[18] In summary, vv. 21–24, less 22aα, form a complete statement in themselves without the following vv. 25–27.[19]

TEXT AND TRANSLATION

21 שָׂנֵאתִי מָאַסְתִּי חַגֵּיכֶם וְלֹא אָרִיחַ בְּעַצְּרֹתֵיכֶם:

22 וּמִנְחֹתֵיכֶם לֹא אֶרְצֶה וְשֶׁלֶם[a] מְרִיאֵיכֶם לֹא אַבִּיט:

23 הָסֵר[b] מֵעָלַי[c] הֲמוֹן שִׁרֶיךָ וְזִמְרַת נְבָלֶיךָ לֹא אֶשְׁמָע:

24 וְיִגַּל כַּמַּיִם מִשְׁפָּט וּצְדָקָה כְּנַחַל אֵיתָן:

21 "I hate, I reject your feasts, nor even will I take delight in your solemn assemblies.

22 And your grain offerings, I will not accept them; and any peace offering[a] of your fatted animals I will not look upon.

16. Wolff, *Joel and Amos*, 261; Jeremias, *Amos*, 101.

17. Wolff, *Joel and Amos*, 265; Jeremias, *Amos*, 101. For a dissenting opinion, see Paul, *Amos*, 190.

18. Wolff, *Joel and Amos*, 259; Jeremias, *Amos*, 106. See 1 Chr 16:2, 40; 21:24, 26; 23:31; 29:21; 2 Chr 1:6; 8:12; 23:18; 24:14; 29:7, 27; 35:14, 16; Ezra 3:3, 6.

19. Mays, *Amos*, 110; Wolff, *Joel and Amos*, 261; Jeremias, *Amos*, 101. For an opposing argument, see Andersen and Freedman (*Amos*, 141) who conclude that "there is no surefire technique for distinguishing authentic Amos materials from the additions of later scribes." Nevertheless, this author denies vv. 22aα and 25–27 to Amos and attributes them to at least one later redactor, but probably more.

a. The word, וְשֶׁלֶם, "and any peace offering," is a *hapax legomenon* in the singular. The

23 "Remove^b from me^c your noisy songs; I will not even listen to the melody of your lyres.

24 "But let justice flow like water, and righteousness like a perennial *wadi*.

FORM CRITICISM

The literary form of the text is a first person divine speech that may be structured thus:[20]

vv. 21–23 Rejection of worship (assemblies, sacrifice, and prayer)

plural is expected because the other offerings in this unit are in the plural (Andersen and Freedman, *Amos*, 527; Wolff, *Joel and Amos*, 263; also Driggers, "Israel," 28). Without the conjunction, שְׁלָמִים is used twenty-two times: Gen 34:21; Exod 24:5; 32:6; Lev 3:1, 6; 17:5; 19:5; 22:21; 23:19; Num 6:17; 15:8; Deut 27:7; Josh 8:31; 22:23; 1 Sam 10:8; 11:15; 1 Kgs 3:15; 2 Chr 30:22; 33:16; Prov 7:14; Ezek 46:12; Nah 1:12. With the conjunction, וּשְׁלָמִים is used seven times: Judg 20:26; 21:4; 2 Sam 6:17; 24:25; 1 Kgs 9:25; 1 Chr 16:1; 21:26. The *BHS* apparatus shows that some mss read וְשַׁלְמֵי, the plural construct, but, given the context, such an emendation is unnecessary. Driggers ("Israel," 28 n. 12) suggests that the final ם may have been dropped due to haplography with the following word מְרִיאֵיכֶם. The lack of a definite article and the use of the singular form suggest the reference is to *any* peace offering that the people may offer (Joüon, *Grammar*, 510).

b. The abrupt change from plural suffixes (vv. 21–22) to singular suffix endings, coupled with a singular imperative verb, הָסֵר, "remove," in v. 23 signifies a change in focus from general and public forms of worship to specific and individual practices (Paul, *Amos*, 191). This change is evident from the fact that the offerings and sacrifices were products of the land, whereas music and singing were gifts of individual people (even if those individuals joined together as choirs do) (Driggers, "Israel," 29). Amos 6:5; 8:3, 10 show that music and songs were integral parts of temple worship (Andersen and Freedman, *Amos*, 527–8). *BHS* proposes a plural imperative, הָסִירוּ, in v. 23, but this is unnecessary because there are numerous examples in prophetic literature of singular verbs being used in place of the plural (Paul, *Amos*, 191; Andersen and Freedman, *Amos*, 528). Wolff (*Joel and Amos*, 259) notes (and Andersen and Freedman [*Amos*, 528] agree) the possibility that the verb was originally an infinitive absolute, as is קַטֵּר, "burn," in Amos 4:5, and that the objects in v. 23 with their plural suffixes have been syntactically misunderstood and so changed to second person singular pronominal suffixes, שִׁרֶיךָ, "your songs," and נְבָלֶיךָ, "your lyres," at a later time. The critical apparatus in *BHS* notes the possibility that second person plural pronominal suffixes were secondarily affixed to the terms for "songs" and "lyres," thus resulting in שִׁירֵיכֶם and נִבְלֵיכֶם, but this is unnecessary.

c. The use of the indirect object following the imperative, מֵעָלַי, literally "from upon me," implies that the objects to be removed are physically weighing upon Yhwh (Weiss, "Cult," 207). See a parallel idea in Isa 1:14.

20. Wolff, *Joel and Amos*, 260; Andersen and Freedman, *Amos*, 523; Paul, *Amos*, 188; Jeremias, *Amos*, 101; Mays, *Amos*, 106, 110.

v. 24   Resolution proposed

BHS displays the text of vv. 21–24 in poetic form in which all the verses appear as bi-cola.

STRUCTURE OF THE TEXT

The first person divine speech used in vv. 21–24 sets it apart from the woe oracles that precede (5:18–20) and follow (6:1–7).[21] Additionally, the elimination of the elements attributed above to later redactors (vv. 22aα and 25–27; see above) leaves a four verse bi-cola oracle, all of whose components feature strict parallelism, in which Yhwh speaks directly to the people.[22] The four verses may be divided into a pair of two-verse halves that comprise a cultic decision or response (vv. 21–22) and an instruction (vv. 23–24), identified as such by its imperative verb + consequences structure.[23] In the prophetic writings, in a negative cultic decision, it is always Yhwh who speaks, according to Wolff, as may be seen in Isa 1:10–17; Jer 6:19–21; and Mal 1:10.[24]

The text features a progression in the divine rejection of Israel's cult that moves from the general celebration of festivals and assemblies (v. 21) to the specific activities involved: sacrifices (v. 22) and singing with musical accompaniment (v. 23). Verse 24 presents the alternative activity that Yhwh expects instead of those he has rejected.

Syntactically, the Hebrew of v. 24 is an ABB′A′ chiasm:

A. water – מַיִם
   B. justice – מִשְׁפָּט
   B′. righteousness – צְדָקָה
A′. wadi – נַחַל

The poetic structure of v. 24 is the key to understanding the importance of the paired terms (justice and righteousness) required of the people. The Israelites are called to let justice *and* righteousness flow like abundant water. These terms are used together forty times in the

21. Paul, *Amos*, 188; Wolff, *Joel and Amos*, 260.

22. Mays, *Amos*, 106; Wolff, *Joel and Amos*, 260–61.

23. Wolff, *Joel and Amos*, 261; Andersen and Freedman, *Amos*, 523. See Amos 4:4–5.

24. Wolff (*Joel and Amos*, 261) continues, "One can assume that, within the context of a ritual of lamentation, a cultic spokesman gave voice to Yahweh's word."

OT, with Amos himself using the combination three times (here and in 5:7 and 6:12).[25] The phrase "justice and righteousness" refers not to behavioral goals, but to primary gifts that Yhwh has granted the people and that they, in turn, should allow to flourish, just as abundant water enables the land to flourish.[26]

AUTHENTICITY AND DATING

Scholars agree in their attribution of vv. 21–24 to the eighth-century prophet Amos.[27] Wolff dates the text more specifically to about 760 BC, using the archaeological evidence of an earthquake in Hazor to determine the unit's more exact time period.[28] Paul says that Amos had to have finished his prophetic mission by 745 BC because his book makes no reference to the economic downturn that followed the death of Jeroboam II or to the threat of the Assyrians.[29] Since scholars generally acknowledge Amos's authorship of vv. 21–24, there is no compelling reason for me to claim otherwise. The dating of the archaeological finds at Hazor and the lack of reference to the economic problems following the death of Jeroboam II allow for outside dates of 760–745 BC for Amos's prophetic mission.

THE UNIT IN ITS CONTEXT

Andersen and Freedman understand vv. 21–24 as part of the larger segment 5:16–27, which joins together originally separate units via an inclusion that begins with לָכֵן כֹּה־אָמַר יְהוָה אֱלֹהֵי צְבָאוֹת, "Therefore, thus

25. Outside Amos, the word pair *justice and righteousness*, occurs in: Gen 18:19; 1 Kgs 10:9; 2 Chr 9:8; Job 29:14; 37:23; Pss 33:5; 72:1, 2; 89:14; 97:2; 99:4; 106:3; Prov 1:3; 2:9; 8:20; 21:3; Eccl 3:16; Isa 1:21, 27; 5:7, 16; 9:7; 28:17; 32:1, 16; 33:5; 59:9, 14; Jer 9:24; 22:3, 15; 23:5; 33:15; Hos 2:19; Wis 5:18; 8:7; and 1 Macc 2:29.

26. Jeremias, *Amos*, 104.

27. Auld, *Amos*, 65; Mays, *Amos*, 113; Jeremias, *Amos*, 105–106; Andersen and Freedman, *Amos*, 144; Wolff, *Joel and Amos*, 120, 262; Paul, *Amos*, 6.

28. Wolff (*Joel and Amos*, 262) notes that Stratum VI at Hazor shows destruction believed to have been caused by an earthquake, possibly the one to which Amos 1:1 refers, that can be dated to about 760 BC.

29. Paul, *Amos*, 1.

says Yhwh, God of hosts," in 5:16a and ends with the similar expression אָמַר יְהוָה אֱלֹהֵי־צְבָאוֹת, "Says Yhwh, God of hosts," in 5:27b.[30] Andersen and Freedman credit a later editor with drawing together the originally unrelated component units in this segment.[31] The context of which 5:21–24 is a part consists therefore of an opening oracle (5:16–17) that introduces the concept of a future visitation of Yhwh that will result in judgment of the people, and continues with a woe oracle concerning the Day of Yhwh (5:18–20).[32] The editor who joined together the warning of vv. 16–17 and the woe oracle of vv. 18–20 probably conceived the two units as warnings of the same event.[33] The third and final section of the unit is vv. 21–27,[34] in which the editor who joined the three units together may also have been responsible for the addition of vv. 22aα, and 25–27. The last section (5:21–27) fits into the larger unit because it continues the preceding warning by rejecting Israel's cultic activities (vv. 21–23), summarizes the true goal of Israelite society (v. 24), then connects the period of the Wilderness Wanderings to Israel's current illicit sacrificial activities (vv. 25–26), and finally threatens exile (v. 27) should the audience not respond appropriately.[35]

EXEGETICAL ANALYSIS

Verse 21

The verse opens with two verbs juxtaposed asyndetically in first person address with "your feasts" as object.[36] Although the verb שָׂנֵא, "to hate," usually takes a human direct object, Yhwh is rarely said to hate people (Hos 9:15; Mal 1:13; Pss 11:5; 31:7); things or abstract qualities are more often the object of God's hatred (Isa 61:8; Jer 44:4; Deut 12:31; Zech 8:17).[37]

30. Andersen and Freedman, *Amos*, 537.

31. Ibid.

32. Ibid. Mays (*Amos*, 96–99), on the contrary, joins vv. 16–17 to vv. 13–14 as a single unit.

33. Andersen and Freedman, *Amos*, 538.

34. Ibid.

35. Andersen and Freedman, *Amos*, 542–44; Mays, *Amos*, 110–13.

36. Paul, *Amos*, 189; Wolff, *Joel and Amos*, 258; Weiss, "Cult," 203.

37. Andersen and Freedman, *Amos*, 525–26. Lipinski ("שָׂנֵא," 14. 164–74) provides a complete list of the specific behaviors that Yhwh "hates" (167).

There are only four other places in the OT in which Yhwh is the first-person subject of the verb, שָׂנֵאתִי, "I hate."[38] The second verb form, מָאַסְתִּי, "I reject," in v. 21 is only used two other times in the OT, both times by Job when speaking in his own defense.[39] Such strong words, used without a conjunction, are meant to impress upon the people the revulsion with which Yhwh views the activities mentioned in the verses that follow.[40] These are the only affirmative verbs in the passage.[41]

After the foregoing positive verbs, there is a conjunction plus negative particle combination, וְלֹא, which I have translated "nor even." This translation seems appropriate because the combination opens a phrase that continues the train of thought begun by the preceding verbs that express negative emotions and serves to intensify the phrase that follows.[42]

The use of the second person plural pronominal suffixes in v. 21 in connection with pilgrimage feasts and solemn assemblies, that is, to activities that required cessation of work and travel to a specified location, recalls the conversation in Exod 32:7–11 in which Yhwh and Moses each claim that the people belongs to the other.[43] Additionally, the Israelite feasts are ascribed to the people, rather than to God, only two other times in the OT.[44]

---

38. Of these instances, only Mal 1:3 has a person for the direct object (Esau). The other three cases are Jer 44:4 (this abominable deed); Amos 6:8 (his citadels); and Zec 8:17 (all these things).

39. Job 7:16 reads, מָאַסְתִּי לֹא־לְעֹלָם אֶחְיֶה חֲדַל מִמֶּנִּי כִּי־הֶבֶל יָמָי, "I reject, I will not live forever, leave me alone, for my days are a breath," and 30:1 reads: וְעַתָּה שָׂחֲקוּ עָלַי צְעִירִים מִמֶּנִּי לְיָמִים אֲשֶׁר־מָאַסְתִּי אֲבוֹתָם לָשִׁית עִם־כַּלְבֵי צֹאנִי, "And now those who are younger than me laugh at me, whose fathers I rejected, for I put them with the dogs of my flock." Andersen and Freedman (*Amos,* 526) say that the opposite term, i.e., בָּחַר, indicates divine choice, as in Deut 7:6.

40. Weiss, "Cult," 203; Mays, *Amos,* 106.

41. Weiss, "Cult," 203.

42. *HALOT* 1:257 notes the conjunction ו may emphasize what follows. See also Waltke and O'Connor, *Syntax,* 649.

43. Mays, *Amos,* 106–7.

44. Amos 8:10 reads, וְהָפַכְתִּי חַגֵּיכֶם לְאֵבֶל וְכָל־שִׁירֵיכֶם לְקִינָה, "I will turn your feasts into mourning and all your songs into dirges," and Mal 2:3 reads, הִנְנִי גֹעֵר לָכֶם אֶת־הַזֶּרַע וְזֵרִיתִי פֶרֶשׁ עַל־פְּנֵיכֶם פֶּרֶשׁ חַגֵּיכֶם וְנָשָׂא אֶתְכֶם אֵלָיו, "Behold, I will rebuke your offspring, and I will spread manure on your faces, the manure of your feasts, and you will be carried off with it." Also, Nah 2:1, using the singular, refers to "your feasts" in an address to Judah, while Yhwh refers to these feasts in the first person singular in Exod 23:18 when he provides instructions for the three annual feasts: לֹא־תִזְבַּח עַל־חָמֵץ דַּם־זִבְחִי וְלֹא־יָלִין חֵלֶב־חַגִּי עַד־בֹּקֶר, "You

Verse 22

The repetition of the second person plural pronominal suffix reinforces the rejection: even if *you* offer *your* grain offerings, *I* (Yhwh) reject them. The text clearly distinguishes the action of the audience from the reaction of the speaker via its use of such grammatical devices. The book of Amos employs second person plural suffixes a second time (8:10) in another speech attributed to Yhwh.[45] The association of offerings with the people is not as such unusual in the OT. Feast days, sacrifices, incense, new moons, Sabbaths, and solemn assemblies are often mentioned in connection with the use of the suffixes כֶם־, "your," or הָ־, "her," with the pronouns referring to the people, to Zion, or to Judah.[46] Although biblical texts make use of the second person pronominal suffix in reference to cultic activities and festival celebrations, Amos's use of the suffix signifies a disconnect between the people's celebrations and Yhwh.[47] The people's celebrations are not having any positive effect on God whenever Amos calls them "yours."[48]

The two verbs used in this verse help in determining the meaning of the unit as a whole. The first, אֶרְצֶה (לֹא), "I will (not) accept," is the ordinary, and most frequently used, term for the acceptance or rejection of a sacrificial gift.[49] The root רצה is frequently employed in Leviticus when the priest, the officiant at the sacrifice, declares whether an animal of sacrifice or some specific ritual action associated with rituals is or is not acknowledged by Yhwh.[50] A major difference between the priestly use of the verb in Leviticus and Yhwh's use of it

---

shall not offer with leavened bread the blood of my sacrifice, and the fat of my feast shall not remain overnight until morning."

45. Paul, *Amos*, 263. See n. 44 for text of Amos 8:10.

46. Jeremias, *Amos*, 103. Although not exhaustive, the following list exemplifies the use of the pronouns "your" in reference to sacrifices: Nah 2:1; Jer 6:20; Isa 1:11, 13, 14; Mal 2:3; and "her": Lam 1:4; Hos 2:13. At other times, feasts are called חַגֵּי־יהוה, "feasts of Yhwh": Exod 10:9; Lev 23:39; Judg 21:19; Hos 9:5.

47. Jeremias, *Amos*, 103.

48. Ibid.

49. Paul, *Amos*, 190; Jeremias, *Amos*, 102. Paul and Jeremias list several texts where this term is used to signify acceptance of a sacrifice by the priest speaking on behalf of Yhwh, e.g., Lev 1:3–4; 19:7; 22:23, 25, 27; Jer 14:12; Ezek 20:41; Hos 8:13; Mal 1:10; 2:13; Ps 51:18.

50. Jeremias, *Amos*, 102. See Lev 1:3–4; 7:18; 19:5–7; 22:19, 20, 23, 25, 27, 29; 23:11.

here in Amos is that, while the priest issues a ruling on an individual gift, animal, or prayer, Yhwh rejects Israel's entire ritual activity, and does so using traditional cul̹tic vocabulary.[51] After Yhwh's first negative statement there follows his rejection of peace offerings and fatted animals: לֹא אַבִּיט, "I will not look upon." According to Paul, the root נבט is never used, except here, in a cultic context.[52] The use of the above verbs recalls the phrase, וְלֹא אָרִיחַ, in v. 21, with its connotation of "(not) accepting." Yhwh does not assent to the people's sacrifices nor does he look upon them. In both cases, the roots נבט and רוח fit the context: they expand the idea of v. 21, such that God now uses his sense of sight to signify his refusal of the gifts of the people.

Verse 23

The only imperative verb in this pericope, הָסֵר, is addressed to the musicians and singers, who are not only instructed to cease their worthless activities, but also are told to remove all vestiges of sound from Yhwh's presence.[53] This verse represents the third time Yhwh invokes human senses in rebuffing temple activities: he will not smell (v. 21), see (v. 22), or hear (v. 23). By the end of v. 23, Yhwh has categorically refused to participate in worship at Bethel.[54]

Yhwh commands the people to remove their music and singing מֵעָלַי, "from upon me," thus suggesting that the weight of songs and music are heavy objects that are a burden to him. The first object used, שִׁרֶיךָ, "your songs," appears with the singular masculine construct noun modifier, הֲמוֹן, "noisy." The meaning of הֲמוֹן can range from "murmur" to "tumult," but the allusion here, given the association with singing, is to

---

51. Jeremias, *Amos*, 102–3.

52. Paul, *Amos*, 190. In Gen 4:4–5 God שָׁעָה, "looks upon," Abel's gift with favor, but לֹא שָׁעָה, "does not look upon," Cain's gift thus.

53. According to 1 Chr 6:16–32; 15:16–22; and 25:1–31, David appointed certain Levites at the (Jerusalem) Temple as musicians and for choir services. Although these texts postdate the time of Amos, the tradition probably does not. According to 1 Kgs 12:31, Jeroboam appointed his own priests to serve the northern temples in Dan and Bethel וַיַּעַשׂ אֶת־בֵּית בָּמוֹת וַיַּעַשׂ כֹּהֲנִים מִקְצוֹת הָעָם אֲשֶׁר לֹא־הָיוּ מִבְּנֵי לֵוִי, "And he built temples on the high places, and he made priests from among the people, who were not from the sons of Levi."

54. Mays, *Amos*, 106.

the volume of the songs.[55] Under normal circumstances the singing of שִׁירִים, "songs" (of praise), to Yhwh was considered a good thing through-out the various periods of Israel's history.[56] At other times, Yhwh turns songs into laments, as in the case in Amos 8:10. Yhwh may also call for an end to such singing, as happens in Amos 5:23 and Ezek 26:13.[57] The sound of singing that the people associated with liturgical worship is ill-received by Yhwh who instructs them to cease that activity.

The second burdensome object for Yhwh is וְזִמְרַת נְבָלֶיךָ, "even the melody of your lyres." This phrase begins with an emphatic *waw* which states that Yhwh will not listen to the people's songs or "even" to their music.[58] Weiss points out that the root זמר refers not to songs per se, but rather to the playing of notes; thus the noun זִמְרָה suggests the music or melody that is played.[59] As was the case with the people's songs, in its normal use this term refers to praise of Yhwh.[60] The term נֵבֶל is employed also in Amos 6:5 and Isa 5:12; 14:11. These four occurrences indicate that the term denotes an instrument used to play music for entertainment at secular or at religious feasts, such as worship in the temples.[61] Wolff explains that the lyre was the oldest and most impor-tant stringed instrument in Israel, and that it could have as many as ten strings.[62] In any case, the playing of a lyre, as David did to soothe Saul (1 Sam 16:23), is rejected by Yhwh.

55. Weiss, "Cult," 207. Wolff (*Joel and Amos*, 263) notes the use of this word in 1 Kgs 20:13 in reference to the din of battle. 1 Kgs 20:13 reads: וְהִנֵּה נָבִיא אֶחָד נִגַּשׁ אֶל־אַחְאָב מֶלֶךְ־יִשְׂרָאֵל וַיֹּאמֶר כֹּה אָמַר יְהוָה הֲרָאִיתָ אֵת כָּל־הֶהָמוֹן הַגָּדוֹל הַזֶּה הִנְנִי נֹתְנוֹ בְיָדְךָ הַיּוֹם וְיָדַעְתָּ כִּי־אֲנִי יְהוָה "And behold, one prophet drew near to Ahab, king of Israel and said, 'Thus says Yhwh: Do you see all this great turmoil? Behold, I will give them into your hand and you shall know that I am Yhwh.'"

56. A short list of OT texts that mention singing hymns of praise to God includes: Gen 31:27; Exod 15:1; Num 21:17; 1 Sam 18:6; 1 Chr 13:8; 2 Chr 5:13; Neh 12:27; Job 36:24; Pss 13:6; 33:3; Isa 26:1; and Jer 20:13.

57. Ezek 26:13 reads: וְהִשְׁבַּתִּי הֲמוֹן שִׁירָיִךְ וְקוֹל כִּנּוֹרַיִךְ לֹא יִשָּׁמַע עוֹד, "I will remove the sound of your songs, and the sound of your lyres will not be heard again." The negative counter-part of the שִׁירִים, "songs of praise," is קִינִים, "laments" or "mourning songs." Among refer-ences to laments are Amos 5:1; 8:10; 2 Sam 1:17; 2 Chr 35:25; Jer 7:29; and Ezek 26:17.

58. See n. 42.

59. Weiss, "Cult," 208.

60. See also 1 Chr 16:9; Pss 9:12; 30:5; Isa 12:5.

61. Weiss, "Cult," 208.

62. Wolff, *Joel and Amos*, 264. A lyre had an angular yoke and a bulging resonance chamber. Mays (*Amos*, 107) notes that archaeologists have found depictions of lyres at

Verse 24

The conjunctive *waw* that begins the clause when it precedes a jussive verb expresses contrast, "but," because the following positive clause reverses the tone set by the negative clauses of vv. 21–23.[63] This contrast, combined with the jussive verb to which ו is attached, generates a command by Yhwh for the people to take a specific action.[64] The jussive form of the verb emphasizes the contrast with the message of the three preceding verses.[65] The objects of this verb, justice and righteousness, are inanimate. This combination (jussive plus non-animate objects) places a greater emphasis on the task at hand than on those who are to accomplish it.[66]

The verb יִגַּל, "let roll," anticipates the water-based similes that follow. The root גלל is the root of other Hebrew "water" words, such as גַּל, "wave" (Isa 51:15; Jer 5:22; Ezek 26:3; Job 38:11; Jonah 2:4; Zech 10:11; and Ps 42:8); גַּל, "fountain" (Song 4:12); and גֻּלָּה, "spring" (Josh 15:19; Eccl 12:6).[67] The use of this verb also looks forward to the action in v. 27, where Yhwh הִגְלֵיתִי, "will lead into exile," a form of the homonymous root גלה.[68]

The familiar collocation that follows the verb is presented as a pair of similes: כַמַּיִם מִשְׁפָּט וּצְדָקָה כְּנַחַל אֵיתָן, "justice like water; and righteousness like a perennial *wadi*." Although Amos is the first to use this simile, Second Isaiah uses a similar one.[69] All of Israel's feasts, assemblies, offerings, and music are, the verse is saying, to flow out of

---

many archaeological sites.

63. Weiss, "Cult," 209; Paul, *Amos*, 192 n. 47; Waltke and O'Connor, *Syntax*, 129, 677.

64. Driggers, "Israel," 31; Jeremias, *Amos*, 104. Waltke and O'Connor (*Syntax*, 568) say that a jussive emanating from a superior, in this case Yhwh, to an inferior, the people, has the force of a command. Berquist ("Dangerous Waters," 56) discusses the possibility of reading the jussive as an imperfect, "Justice will roll."

65. Driggers, "Israel," 31.

66. Waltke and O'Connor, *Syntax*, 570; Driggers, "Israel," 31; Berquist, "Dangerous Waters," 56.

67. Paul, *Amos*, 192.

68. Driggers ("Israel," 33) speaks of a thematic connection between the two verbs: they both exemplify the same divine judgment.

69. Andersen and Freedman, *Amos*, 540. Isa 48:18 reads: לוּא הִקְשַׁבְתָּ לְמִצְוֹתָי וַיְהִי כַנָּהָר שְׁלוֹמֶךָ וְצִדְקָתְךָ כְּגַלֵּי הַיָּם, "If only you would pay attention to my commandments, your prosperity would be like a river; and your righteousness like the waves of the sea."

the consistent practice of justice *and* righteousness within the community.[70] Of the three verses in the book of Amos that refer to justice and righteousness, only in this one is a positive command involved. Both Amos 5:7 and 6:12, by contrast, voice similar critiques of the lack of right judgment in community affairs, but have in view the exact opposite meaning of the message in 5:24 because the people perverted justice and rejected righteousness.[71]

A message from God calling for מִשְׁפָּט וּצְדָקָה, "justice and righteousness," is not unique to Amos, but is rather a common biblical theme.[72] However, only in Amos 5:24 and Jer 22:3 is a command given to all the people to practice justice and righteousness.[73] In Gen 18:17–19, Yhwh reflects on whether he should inform Abraham of the imminent destruction of Sodom and Gomorrah, and God directs Abraham to instruct his children and posterity to keep the ways of Yhwh by doing what is right and just. In Deut 16:18, Yhwh instructs Moses to appoint judges who will administer righteous judgment. In 1 Kgs 10:9 and 2 Chr 9:8 the king receives praise from the queen of Sheba because Yhwh gave him authority to administer with justice and righteousness. Other OT passages that instruct the people to seek justice include Hos 10:12; Isa 51:1; Zeph 2:3; and Wis 1:1. Ezekiel presents מִשְׁפָּט וּצְדָקָה as an option available to the wicked man to turn from his evil ways so that he might live.[74] Finally, there are several references in the OT that affirm that obedience is preferable to sacrifice.[75]

The notion that justice and righteousness are required of the people is reflected in the people's constant request of Yhwh that he

---

70. Jeremias, *Amos*, 104; Mays, *Amos*, 108.

71. Andersen and Freedman, *Amos*, 528; Mays, *Amos*, 108; Jeremias, *Amos*, 104.

72. The phrase מִשְׁפָּט וּצְדָקָה, appears 22 times in the OT: 2 Sam 8:15; 1 Kgs 10:9; 1 Chr 18:14; 2 Chr 9:8; Ps 99:4; Isa 32:16; 33:5; 59:14; Jer 9:23; 22:3, 15; 23:5; 33:15; Ezek 18:5, 19, 21, 27; 33:14, 16, 19, Amos 5:7, 24.

73. Jer 22:3 reads, כֹּה אָמַר יְהֹוָה עֲשׂוּ מִשְׁפָּט וּצְדָקָה וְהַצִּילוּ גָזוּל מִיַּד עָשׁוֹק וְגֵר יָתוֹם וְאַלְמָנָה אַל־תֹּנוּ אַל־תַּחְמֹסוּ וְדָם נָקִי אַל־תִּשְׁפְּכוּ בַּמָּקוֹם הַזֶּה, "Thus says Yhwh, 'Do justice and righteousness, and deliver the one who was robbed from his oppressor; and do not oppress or treat violently the sojourner, the orphan, or the widow; and do not shed innocent blood in this place.'"

74. Ezek 18:5, 19, 21, 27; 33:14, 16, 19.

75. Hos 6:6; Jer 7:3–6; 1 Sam 15:22; Pss 33:5; 103:6; Prov 21:3; Isa 58:6–11; and Eccl 12:13.

judge between them and whichever foreign nation happens to be threatening them at the moment. If the people expect Yhwh to act in their favor, they too are required to act justly towards each other. Throughout the Psalms there are examples of the call for Yhwh to vindicate the Israelites because of their own righteousness in relation to their enemies, or declarations of Yhwh's justice and righteousness in the way he deals with people.[76]

The two kinds of water mentioned in Amos 5:24 evoke different images. The first, מַיִם, "water," is a generic term that is used to describe both the sea and fresh water.[77] Such water could be inside or outside of Israel.[78] The image is of a major body of water that does not dry up or evaporate. Jeremiah uses the term in an opposite sense in 15:18, when he speaks of a אַכְזָב מַיִם, "deceptive stream" whose water is unreliable.

The second term, נַחַל, "wadi," when used without any geographic site name, refers to the water that appears during the rainy season and dries up during the summer, leaving only the deep crevice cut by the flow of water until the next rainy season.[79] The *wadi* contrasts with the נָהָר, a "river," which never dries up. נָהָר is never used to designate any waterway in Israel itself.[80] The only other place the phrase, נַחַל אֵיתָן is used in the OT is in Deut 21:4, where it seems to refer to regularly running water, as in a stream or river.

Amos, the former farmer and shepherd, uses an image in v. 24 that would be familiar to those living in an arid climate. Whether the people were engaged in tending their fields or flocks, water was a necessity to them. In many texts, Yhwh's action of providing rain at the proper time

---

76. Pss 3:8; 17:2; 31:1; 43:1; 71:2 are some examples of psalms requesting vindication against unjust enemies. Pss 5:9; 9:5; 19:9; 109:31; 119:137 are references to Yhwh's justice and righteousness in his dealing with people.

77. Clements, "מַיִם," 8. 269.

78. Ibid.

79. Snijders ("נַחַל," 9. 336–7) asserts that to translate the term אֵיתָן as "constant" or "ever-flowing" in Amos 5:24 is a contradiction in terms, "because it is characteristic of a *naḥal* to flow only sporadically." He suggests that, by definition, a *wadi* cannot flow permanently, so "the expression [*naḥal ʾēṯān*] probably describes a devastating torrent," one whose powerful flow best accords with Amos's image. According to *ABD* 6. 683, geographic names appearing with the element *wadi* refer to rivers, as in נַחַל אַרְנֹן, *Wadi* Arnon (Deut 2:24) or נַחַל יַבֹּק, *Wadi* Jabbok, (Deut 2:37).

80. Snijders et al., "נָהָר," 9. 264. Snijders also notes that the only river in Israel is always referred to in the OT simply as יַרְדֵּן, "Jordan."

is associated with right behavior.[81] In other passages, water (rain, dew) is used as a metaphor for justice.[82] The association of bountiful, everlasting water with the practice of righteousness and justice provides a clear illustration of the kind of worship Yhwh demands.

In its use of both terms, מַיִם and נַחַל, the text presents an image that suggests life and fertility rather than the death and violence involved in sacrifice.[83] The image of a permanent body of water, followed by a reference to a *wadi* that never dries up, reflects the Israelite understanding of justice and righteousness throughout the OT. Justice and righteousness, when practiced, create good for the community.[84] In the OT, there is no concept of being only partly righteous or achieving certain levels of justice.[85] The community, and the individuals within it, lived righteousness and justice, or they did not.[86]

Thus, v. 24 informs the audience of the purpose of Yhwh's foregoing criticism of Israel's worship. Amos has built up to this point (vv. 21–23) by spelling out Yhwh's reasons for the message that he presents in this verse. The missing element in the Israelite community is the reason for Yhwh's anger. Both physically, in the form of plenty of fresh flowing water, and figuratively, in the form of justice and righteousness within the community, Yhwh defines the situation as he sees it: the people have fallen short of his expectations of acting with justice and righteousness by the way they mistreat the less fortunate in their community. Yhwh rejects the performance of public displays of worship and festive assemblies that the people perceive as fulfilling their devotional obligation to God.[87]

---

81. Deut 11:13–15; 28:12; 1 Kgs 8:35–36.

82. Psalm 72; Hos 6:3; 14:5–7.

83. Wolff, *Joel and Amos*, 112, 264. See also the discussion of sacrifice as an act of violence in Girard, *Violence*; Burkert, *Homo Necans*.

84. See, e.g., Exod 23:6; Lev 24:22; Num 35:29; Deut 16:18; 2 Sam 8:15; 1 Kgs 3:6.

85. Jeremias, *Amos*, 104.

86. Ibid. See Amos 5:7, 11–12; 6:12.

87. Weiss (*Cult*, 213) says: "What cannot be determined . . . is the the [*sic*] actual intent of the polemic: was it aimed at cultic activity in general as a manifestation of worship or at some specific cult? Is the negation made only in principle, or is it intended to be put into practice?" To extend Weiss's questions further: is Amos's extreme form of sarcasm intended to make the people behave differently even as they continue to perform the duties of the cult? Weiss ends his discussion with the statement: "It may even be worthwhile to consider the possibility that the absolute negation of the cultic acts witnessed

SUMMARY

Some scholars cite Amos 5:21–24 as evidence of an eighth-century pro-phetic anti-cultic attitude.[88] Other scholars argue that Amos was not interested in completely eliminating the cult.[89] Sacrifice was not bad, in and of itself, but neither was it necessary in order to maintain one's standing with God.[90]

Andersen and Freedman find it hard to believe that any ancient Israelite would seriously call for abolishing the regular or festival cer-emonies, especially of the various ritual actions performed at those times.[91] But the practice of "worship" is not what Amos is criticizing. Rather, the priority given by his hearers to performing cultic activities at the temple over other forms of living out one's proper bond with Yhwh was the problem. Justice and righteousness in the people's lives, hospi-tality toward their neighbors, right judgments at the city gates, proper weights and measures in the markets, these ways of worshipping Yhwh were far more important than offering an unneeded sacrifice.

The image Amos uses is that of flowing water. Justice and righ-teousness are to flow like a perennial *wadi*. To his original audience, this was an analogy that would indeed have resonated with them. They lived in an arid region with the salty Mediterranean Sea and Dead Sea to their west and southeast respectively, the fresh water Sea of Galilee and the Jordan River to their east, and their only other source of fresh water the winter rains that dried up as fast as they came unless they were collected in man-made cisterns and reservoirs.

The Israelites were not to be like the intermittent *wadis* that dried up soon after the rainy season ended. That is, they were not to practice good works only during the festivals, or only when they were at home.

---

by the prophet is in fact merely a 'dialectical negation,' a rhetorical technique employed in order to emphasize with greater force his historically conditioned demand for 'justice and righteousness'" (214).

88. Marti, *Dodekapropheten*, 180, 194; Wellhausen, *Prolegomena*, 56–58; Smith, "Amos," 94–103, 157–87; Weiser, *Prophetie*, 318–19; Robinson, *Prophecy and the Prophets*, 60–71; and Whitley, *Prophetic Achievement*, 52–54, 73–77.

89. Wolfe, *Meet Amos,* 62–69; Pfeiffer, *Introduction*, 580–82; de Vaux, *Ancient Israel*, 414–23; Cripps, *Amos*, xxviii–xxxiii, 338–40; Andersen and Freedman, *Amos*, 539; and Jensen, *Ethical Dimensions*, 85.

90. Jeremias, *Amos*, 103; Mays, *Amos*, 108; Paul, *Amos*, 188.

91. Andersen and Freedman, *Amos*, 539.

The House of Israel was to tend to the needs of all in the community on a daily basis, whenever it encountered a person in need. For this reason a perpetual *wadi* was an apt description of how Yhwh wants them to behave: perpetually, with justice and righteousness as their guidelines.

In the next chapter I will examine Isaiah 1:10–17. The similarities between that text and this one in Amos 5:21–24 could indicate a similar and prior source used by both prophets, or that one prophet knew of and adapted the message of the other. The differences between the two texts may also indicate that the prophets had similar, but independent, messages. After completing my examination of Isaiah 1:10–17, I will explore the vocabulary and themes that both passages share. Then I will discuss the implications of our having two passages from the same time period with such similar messages.

4

Isaiah 1:10–17

INTRODUCTION

IN THIS CHAPTER I will analyze Isaiah 1:10–17. This text has been identified among the finds at Qumran, specifically on the complete scroll of the book of Isaiah (1QIsaᵃ).[1] A significant feature of 1QIsaᵃ is its similarity to the Masoretic Text (MT) in *BHS*.[2] I will provide a verse-by-verse exegesis of the text as found in *BHS*, utilizing the methods of criticism mentioned in my first chapter. The chapter will conclude with a brief summary.

---

1. Martínez and Tigchelaar, *Scrolls*, 1:3–4. Fragments 1–2 of 4QIsaᶠ contain Isa 1:10–16 and frag. 3 continues from Isa 1:18 (1. 265). Fitzmyer (*Responses*, 20) describes 1QIsaᵃ as a scroll containing all 66 chapters of Isaiah, although a few words are missing at the bottom of some columns due to the scroll's decay.

2. Fitzmyer (*Responses*, 20) notes that 1QIsaᵃ has been radiocarbon dated to 202–107 BC. The oldest previously known codex that contains the text of Isaiah was the Cairo Codex of the Former and Latter Prophets, which has been dated to AD 895. Thus, Fitzmyer explains, the thousand year lapse between the two quite similar texts "bears singular testimony to the fidelity with which the book of Isaiah was copied throughout the centuries by Jewish scribes." The only significant difference between the text of Isaiah 1:10–17 in MT and 1QIsaᵃ is discussed below in n. r.

DELIMITATION OF THE TEXT

The book of Isaiah opens with a series of oracles in chap. 1 that draw attention to the state of the relationship between the Israelites and Yhwh,[3] the former's illicit behavior in particular.[4] This chapter will focus on the third oracle (taking 1:2–3 and 1:4–9 as the first two), that is, Isa 1:10–17.[5] The passage opens with a call to attention (v. 10) followed by a divine speech (vv. 11–17).[6] In this text, Yhwh makes a series of accusations that are similar to those made in Amos 5:21–24. While the units in vv. 4–9 and 10–17 reflect two distinct occasions, they are linked because of their common reference to Sodom and Gomorrah.[7] The use of the quotation formula יֹאמַר יְהוָה in v. 11 identifies the verses that follow (vv. 12–17) as the direct speech of Yhwh. The repetition of the same formula in v. 18 signals the start of a new, distinct unit.[8] Specifically, v. 18 begins with the cohortative לְכוּ־נָא, "come now" followed by the legal technical term וְנִוָּכְחָה, "let us argue."[9] When used together the two terms signify a summons to a legal case.[10] The quotation formula יֹאמַר יְהוָה in v. 18

---

3. The opening chapter contains the following six oracles: 1:1–3, 4–9, 10–17, 18–20, 21–28, 29–31. Wildberger, *Isaiah 1–12*, 9, 78–80; Blenkinsopp, *Isaiah 1–39*, 180–81; Kaiser, *Isaiah 1–12*, 10–45; Childs, *Isaiah*, 16; by contrast, Seitz (*Isaiah*, 31–38) views all of chap. 1 as a single vision; Motyer (*Isaiah*, 45–48) regards vv. 10–20 as a unit, while Oswalt (*Isaiah*, 79–102) sees Isa 1:10–17 as part one of a two-part oracle (1:10–20) that concludes with vv. 18–20.

4. Wildberger, *Isaiah 1–12*, 9–52; Blenkinsopp, *Isaiah 1–39*, 188; Motyer, *Isaiah*, 40–52; Kaiser, *Isaiah 1–12*, 24.

5. Isaiah 1:1 is widely recognized as a superscription (Wildberger, *Isaiah 1–12*, 1–2; Blenkinsopp, *Isaiah 1–39*, 175–76; Childs, *Isaiah*, 11; Oswalt, *Isaiah*, 79–83; Sweeney, *Isaiah*, 71; Seitz, *Isaiah*, 22–23), an inscription (Jensen, *Isaiah*, 38–39), a title (Motyer, *Isaiah*, 41–42), a heading (Kaiser, *Isaiah 1–12*, 1–10), or an editorial comment (Brueggemann, *Isaiah*, 11). I agree with these scholars who understand the verse as the later addition by a redactor who understood the verse as an introduction to the entire book (all 66 chapters) rather than simply as an introduction to chap.1.

6. Wildberger, *Isaiah 1–12*, 37–38; Blenkinsopp, *Isaiah 1–39*, 184; Kaiser, *Isaiah 1–12*, 24–25.

7. Wildberger, *Isaiah 1–12*, 36; Childs, *Isaiah*, 19; Sweeney, *Isaiah*, 64; Oswalt, *Isaiah*, 95 n. 12.

8. Wildberger, *Isaiah 1–12*, 36; Blenkinsopp, *Isaiah 1–39*, 184–45; Motyer, *Isaiah*, 45; Kaiser, *Isaiah 1–12*, 25.

9. Wildberger, *Isaiah 1–12*, 36; Childs, *Isaiah*, 20; Sweeney, *Isaiah*, 79, 82; Brueggemann, *Isaiah*, 19; Gray, *Isaiah*, 27.

10. Sweeney, *Isaiah*, 82.

signals the beginning of a unit that ends with the closing formula דָּבָר
כִּי פִּי יְהוָה, "for the mouth of Yhwh has spoken" in v. 20.[11] Yhwh's wholesale rejection of worship in the previous unit (vv. 10–17), that leaves no
opportunity for disputes or counter-arguments, is no longer a topic for
discussion in vv. 18–20. Rather, Yhwh proceeds to settling the matter
legally and reasonably by addressing the issue of Israel's sins apart from
any reference to the worship practices featured in the previous unit.

TEXT AND TRANSLATION

10 שִׁמְעוּ דְבַר־יְהוָה   קְצִינֵי סְדֹם
הַאֲזִינוּ תּוֹרַת אֱלֹהֵינוּ   עַם עֲמֹרָה:
11 לָמָּה־לִּי רֹב־זִבְחֵיכֶם   [a]יֹאמַר יְהוָה
שָׂבַעְתִּי[b] עֹלוֹת אֵילִים   וְחֵלֶב מְרִיאִים
וְדַם פָּרִים וּכְבָשִׂים[d] וְעַתּוּדִים   [c]לֹא חָפָצְתִּי:
12 כִּי תָבֹאוּ לֵרָאוֹת[e] פָּנָי[f]
מִי־בִקֵּשׁ זֹאת[g] מִיֶּדְכֶם   רְמֹס[h] חֲצֵרָי:[i]
13 לֹא תוֹסִיפוּ הָבִיא[j] מִנְחַת־שָׁוְא   קְטֹרֶת תּוֹעֵבָה הִיא לִי[j]
חֹדֶשׁ וְשַׁבָּת[k] קְרֹא מִקְרָא[k]   לֹא־אוּכַל אָוֶן[l] וַעֲצָרָה:[m]
14 חָדְשֵׁיכֶם[n] וּמוֹעֲדֵיכֶם[o]   שָׂנְאָה נַפְשִׁי[p]
הָיוּ עָלַי לָטֹרַח   נִלְאֵיתִי נְשֹׂא:[q]
15 וּבְפָרִשְׂכֶם כַּפֵּיכֶם   אַעְלִים עֵינַי מִכֶּם
גַּם כִּי־תַרְבּוּ תְפִלָּה   אֵינֶנִּי שֹׁמֵעַ יְדֵיכֶם
דָּמִים מָלֵאוּ:[r] 16 רַחֲצוּ הִזַּכּוּ[s]
הָסִירוּ רֹעַ מַעַלְלֵיכֶם   מִנֶּגֶד עֵינָי
חִדְלוּ הָרֵעַ: 17 לִמְדוּ הֵיטֵב
דִּרְשׁוּ מִשְׁפָּט   [t]אַשְּׁרוּ חָמוֹץ[t]
שִׁפְטוּ יָתוֹם   רִיבוּ אַלְמָנָה: ס

10 Hear the word of Yhwh, rulers of Sodom;
listen to the instruction of our God, people of Gomorrah.

---

11. Wildberger, *Isaiah 1–12*, 54.

11 "What are your many sacrifices to me?" ᵃsays Yhwh.ᵃ
"ᵇI am satedᵇ with whole-burnt offerings of rams and fat of fatted animals!
ᶜAnd I am not pleasedᶜ with the blood of bulls ᵈand lambsᵈ and he-goats.
12 "When you come ᵉto appearᵉ before me,ᶠ

a-a. The imperfect tense of יֹאמַר points to Yhwh's consistently "saying"; so used, it occurs only six times in the OT: Isa 1:11, 18; 33:10; 41:21; 66:9; and Ps 12:6. Motyer (*Isaiah*, 46) notes the distinction between this phrase and כֹּה אָמַר יְהוָה, "thus says Yhwh," which recurs 389 times throughout the OT.

b-b. According to Joüon (*Grammar*, 2. 359) this stative verb has a present meaning.

c-c. "Third Isaiah" (Isaiah 56–66) uses the same phrase in 65:12 and 66:4 to express Yhwh's displeasure over some people's behavior, and positively in 56:4 in a description of what a certain group does that pleases Yhwh. Finally, Isa 53:10, uses חָפֵץ to refer to Yhwh's "pleasure" in crushing the Suffering Servant in his iniquity. Motyer, *Isaiah*, 46.

d-d. The word appears in the MT, the Vg and 1QIsaᵃ, but not in the LXX. Wildberger (*Isaiah 1–12*, 34) suggests this word is a scribal addition whose purpose is to ensure a complete listing. Kaiser (*Isaiah 1–12*, 23) sees the term as a disruption in a sequence based on the victims' size, as well as of the "two-membered parallelism" of the previous line. However, given that the word completes the list of animals generally offered in the sacrifices, and, given its presence in all the other versions, I accept it as original.

e-e. One ms and Syr have לִרְאוֹת; this changes the verb from MT's *niphal* (passive = "to be seen," "to appear") to a *qal* (active = "to see"). The LXX reads ὀφθῆναί μοι, "to be seen by me." The Greek reading qualifies the passive verb by indicating who the seer was. Under normal circumstances, the Israelites avoided seeing God, because looking upon God's face would result in death (Gen 16:13; 32:30; Judg 13:22). However, there are instructions for the people to appear before Yhwh: Exod 23:15; 34:23; Deut 16:16; 31:11; 1 Sam 1:22; Pss 42:3; 84:7. It is more acceptable to be seen, than to see. Kaiser (*Isaiah 1–12*, 23) says that MT's reading modified an earlier tradition (as reflected in the passive as in the LXX and the Vg) because by the time of its composition being seen by, rather than seeing, God was more desirable. Bearing in mind, however, that while one should avoid looking upon the face of God, and the Torah does include mandated appearances before him, I accept the MT's current reading.

f. Wildberger (*Isaiah 1–12*, 34) says that a half-verse has dropped out here, which may have read "what do your many offerings accomplish?" On first examination, the verse does appear to lack something, although as it stands the text makes sense.

g. Wildberger (*Isaiah 1–12*, 34) translates זֹאת "such a thing" in anticipation of the following רְמֹס חֲצֵרָי "trampling of my courts" with a deletion of the following מִיֶּדְכֶם, reading literally, "from your hands." He notes that some have proposed replacing מִיֶּדְכֶם with מֵאִתְּכֶם "from you." Finally, he concludes that such an emendation is unnecessary if the זֹאת is understood as a reference back to the missing half verse (see previous note). However, if the verse is translated as it stands, no changes or misunderstandings are evident when one reads מִיֶּדְכֶם as a metonymy in which "hands" represent the whole person, thus, "from you," as in 2 Sam 4:11; Mal 1:9, 10. The only other two OT passages (Mal 1:13; 2:13) that

who seeks this[g] from you, to trample[h] my courts?[i]

13 "No longer bring worthless offerings; incense [j]is an abomination to me![j]

New moon and Sabbath, [k]calling of assembly[k]—I cannot endure the iniquity[l] and the celebration![m]

---

contain this form (מִיֶּדְכֶם) refer literally to something being received "from your hands."

h. 1QIsaᵃ reads לרמוס, "to trample" which likely reflects a scribal attempt to smooth the reading, but this is unnecessary. After having named various animals that were frequently brought to the Temple for sacrificial offerings, Isaiah now draws a parallel between these and the people who also make visits and "trample" Yhwh's courts, a description often related to damage caused by animal movements (2 Kgs 9:33; 14:9; 2 Chr 25:18; Ezek 26:11; 34:18; Dan 8:7, 10; Mic 5:7), although people also trample (2 Kgs 7:17, 20; Ps 7:6; Isa 16:4; 26:6; 28:3; 41:25; Nah 3:14), as does God (Ps 91:13 and Isa 63:3). Motyer, *Isaiah*, 46.

i. Wildberger (*Isaiah 1–12*, 35) notes that the LXX reads τὴν αὐλήν μου, "my court" indicating a single court, rather than the plural, as in the MT. In addition, the phrase is presented in the LXX as part of a clause that begins in v. 12 and ends in v. 13, πατεῖν τὴν αὐλήν μου οὐ προσθήσεσθε, "do not continue to tread about my court." The area in question is mentioned in 2 Kgs 21:5; 23:12; 2 Chr 33:5 as a component of the First Temple in which there were two courts. Ezek 8:16 and 10:5 specifically mention an inner and an outer court in the Temple. The changes in number and word order obscure the meaning that is communicated in the MT, which I retain.

j-j. Wildberger (*Isaiah 1–12*, 35) correctly reads תּוֹעֵבָה הִיא לִי as a relative clause.

k-k. Wildberger (*Isaiah 1–12*, 35) defends the retention of this phrase, based on the meter, and rejects the suggestion that the מִקְרָא, "assembly" is used here as an abbreviation for the postexilic term מִקְרָא־קֹדֶשׁ, "holy assembly." The phrase קְרֹא מִקְרָא sounds alliterative, like "assembling of an assembly," but the English calque is awkward as a translation.

l. Whereas Aquila reads ἀνωφελές, "useless," and Sym and Theod read ἀδικία, "wrongdoing" in their attempt to follow the MT, the LXX renders MT אָוֶן, "iniquity" as νηστεία, "fast," presumably reading Hebrew צוֹם, "fast." Wildberger (*Isaiah 1–12*, 35) regards the MT reading as key to understanding Isaiah's nuanced attitude towards the cult and the activities associated with it, rather than his wholesale rejection of it. He further notes that the concept of fasting did not play an important part in preexilic worship, certainly not on par with festivals and offerings.

m. In the final word of v. 13, 1QIsaᵃ has ועצרתה, "and her celebration," in place of MT's וַעֲצָרָה, "and the celebration." The feminine personal pronoun of the former reading has no referent, so I reject it, and retain the MT text as written. The LXX text of this verse is: οὐ προσθήσεσθε ἐὰν φέρητε σεμίδαλιν μάταιον θυμίαμα βδέλυγμά μοί ἐστιν τὰς νουμηνίας ὑμῶν καὶ τὰ σάββατα καὶ ἡμέραν μεγάλην οὐκ ἀνέχομαι νηστείαν καὶ ἀργίαν, "Stop bringing your useless high-quality flour offerings, incense is loathsome to me; your new moons and Sabbaths and great days - I cannot endure fasting and idleness."

14 "ⁿYour new moonsⁿ and °your annual festivals° I hate to ᵖmy soul.ᵖ

ᑫThey are over me as a burden, and I am weary of carrying them.ᑫ

15 "When you spread out your hands I close my eyes to you,

and if you magnify your prayer, I will not be listening

Your hands are full of blood.ʳ 16 "Wash up!

Clean up!ˢ Remove your evil deeds from my sight.

Cease doing evil. 17 "Learn to do good,

seek justice, ᵗcare for the oppressed,ᵗ

judge for the orphan, defend the widow."

n-n. The text's flow is interrupted by the repetition of a reference to new moons in v. 13b and in 14a. Wildberger (*Isaiah 1–12*, 35) suggests an emendation in this case from חָדְשֵׁיכֶם, "your new moons" to חַגֵּיכֶם, "your (pilgrimage) festivals." Such a reading aligns the text with Hos 2:13 and Ezek 46:11, which both mention a חַג, "pilgrimage festival," and מוֹעֵד, "festivals," while Hosea also includes חֹדֶשׁ, "new moon," and שַׁבָּת, "Sabbath" in the sequence. However, since חַג is not a word commonly used by Isaiah (it appears only twice in 29:1 and 30:29), it is best to leave the text as it stands.

o-o. The text distinguishes between weekly (שַׁבָּת), monthly (חֹדֶשׁ), and annual festivals (מוֹעֵד) by using distinctive terms for each. See Koch, "מוֹעֵד," 8. 167–73, esp. 169–71.

p-p. Concerning Yhwh's נֶפֶשׁ, it is clear that God has no physical (human) attributes such as "life," "self," "soul" or even "throat," the traditional words with which נֶפֶשׁ is usually rendered into English. This is evidenced by the varied ways in which modern authors translate the phrase שָׂנְאָה נַפְשִׁי: "my soul hates" (Kaiser, *Isaiah 1–12*, 24; Jensen, *Isaiah*, 44; Brueggemann, *Isaiah*, 15); "my very being hates" (Oswalt, *Isaiah*, 93); "are absolutely hated by me" (Wildberger, *Isaiah 1–12*, 34); "fill me with revulsion" (Childs, *Isaiah*, 13). Yet, the authors and editors of the OT repeatedly use the term נֶפֶשׁ to describe some characteristic of Yhwh.

q-q. The LXX provides an alternate understanding of the second half of this line: ἐγενήθητέ μοι εἰς πλησμονήν οὐκέτι ἀνήσω τὰς ἁμαρτίας ὑμῶν, "you are no longer producing satisfaction in me, I will abandon your sins," with the sense of letting go of, or dropping, a burden.

r. 1QIsaᵃ adds אצבעותיכם בעאון, "your fingers with iniquity." Wildberger (*Isaiah 1–12*, 36) states that this plus "is the work of a glossator who looked in vain for a mention of fingers at this point." Blenkinsopp (*Isaiah 1–39*, 180) considers the line to be borrowed from Isa 59:3, although he notes its absence from 4QIsaᶠ. The verse in the MT begins with stretching out the palms in prayer and ends with a statement about the blood-covered hands. It presents a complete parallel thought and therefore does not require any further elaboration. For that reason, as well as the fact that the phrase does not appear in any other mss, I retain MT's shorter reading.

s. Wildberger (*Isaiah 1–12*, 36, 48) views this word, in parallel with the one preceding it, as cultic vocabulary because both terms (זכה, רחץ) refer to ethical cleansing as in Ps 51:9.

t-t. The word חָמוֹץ appears only here and in Isa 63:1 in the MT. In the latter chapter

LITERARY FORM

The use of דְּבַר־יְהוָה in v. 10a with תּוֹרַת אֱלֹהֵינוּ in v. 10b identifies the passage as "the instruction of the teacher within the wisdom tradition." [12] These phrases used in connection with the verbs שִׁמְעוּ, "hear," and הַאֲזִינוּ, "listen," serve as a call to attention to the people that is also associated with the wisdom tradition. [13] The introductory phrase: יֹאמַר יְהוָה in vv. 11a identifies what follows as an oracle. [14] The overall literary form of an oracle identifies communication from a god, through an intermediary, such as a priest, seer, or a prophet. [15] Prophetic oracles were based on the prophets' observations of the people's actions. Thus, the text of 1:10–17 is an oracle of Yhwh that reflects the wisdom literature tradition. [16]

---

it refers to the red clothing worn by the one who comes from Edom, while its meaning here in 1:17 is far less clear. *BDB* (p. 330) suggests the meaning "the ruthless," while *HALOT* (1. 327) renders "the oppressor." The phrase in the MT, because it is pointed as an active verb, means "set right the ruthless," i.e., put *them* back on the straight and narrow path. While this is a possible reading, the phrase then throws off the balance of the rest of the verse: in each line the instruction is personal to the one hearing it, and should be acted on by the hearer: *I* should learn to do good, *I* should seek justice, *I* should help the orphan, and *I* should defend the widow. If an I is to do all of these things, I should be the subject of the middle line as well: *I* should come to the aid of the oppressed. The LXX translates the MT's phrase by ῥύσασθε ἀδικούμενον, "rescue those who have been wronged"; the Vg reads *oppresso iudicate*, "judge for the oppressed one." The LXX, Aq, Sym, Theod, and the Vg read the second word, pointed as חָמוֹץ in the MT, as a passive verb that refers to the receiver of the action, "(one who is) oppressed," rather than as חָמוֹץ, which indicates the doer of the action, "oppressor." Such variant readings point out the problems encountered with the phrase even by ancient translators. That an alternative reading is possible also indicates that the problem lies not with the word itself, but with the way that the Masoretes have pointed it. No consonant changes are needed if one simply repoints חָמוֹץ. Therefore, in light of the preceding word, that I translate as "care for," I elect, with Wildberger (*Isaiah 1–12*, 36), Blenkinsopp (*Isaiah 1–39*, 180), Kaiser (*Isaiah 1–12*, 24), and Motyer (*Isaiah*, 47), to repoint the word to reflect a passive sense, thus חָמוֹץ, "care for the oppressed."

12. Jensen, *Use of tôrâ*, 71.

13. Ibid., 69–71.

14. Sweeney (*Isaiah*, 526) defines an oracle as a "broad generic category that designates communication from a deity, often through an intermediary such as a priest, seer, or prophet," as Saul seeks in 1 Sam 28:6: וַיִּשְׁאַל שָׁאוּל בַּיהוָה וְלֹא עָנָהוּ יְהוָה גַּם בַּחֲלֹמוֹת גַּם בָּאוּרִים גַּם בַּנְּבִיאִם: "And Saul consulted Yhwh, but Yhwh gave no answer, neither in dreams, nor by the Urim, nor by the prophets."

15. Sweeney, *Isaiah*, 526.

16. Ibid., 78; Kaiser, *Isaiah 1–12*, 24; Wildberger, *Isaiah 1–12*, 37; and Westermann, *Basic Forms*, 203–5. Other scholars classify the passage as an indictment (Seitz, *Isaiah*,

STRUCTURE OF THE TEXT

As noted above, the text is distinguished from what precedes by its opening call to attention (v. 10) and the quotation formula (יֹאמַר יְהוָה) in v. 11a, and from what follows by a repetition of the same quotation formula (v. 18).[17] The initial verse (v. 10), the call to attention by the prophet, exhibits a three-part parallel structure with the following sequence: imperative verb + object + subject. The references to Sodom and Gomorrah link this verse with v. 9.[18] As with the parallel structure of the call, the audience is addressed in parallel terms.[19] The rulers and the people are named; thus, everyone is included, everyone should listen to what follows. In the next verse Yhwh asks a rhetorical question, then proceeds to answer it (v. 11). The question he asks could reasonably have been posed by anyone who observed Temple activities: why are you doing this? Yhwh structures an answer to his own question in a manner that indicates that he does not appreciate the people's cultic activities, even though his approval is the goal of those actions. After the divine response to the first question, yet another query is presented (v. 12); this delves further into the meaning of Temple practices: who asked you to do this? The answer that follows in the next three verses is arranged in a parallel structure. As a glance at the following chart indicates, in this structure, a command is given, followed by the actions or elements of worship to which the command applies, and finally there is a comment by Yhwh concerning the given action or worship item.

34–35); divine instruction (Blenkinsopp, *Isaiah 1–39*, 180–81); or *tôrâ* instruction (Childs, *Isaiah*, 16).

17. Kugel (*Biblical Poetry*, 30–31) says: "A standard trope of beginning in the Bible is the summoning of the audience's attention, and it is here that one frequently finds the pair 'listen . . . hear.'" See also Kaiser, *Isaiah 1–12*, 25; Motyer, *Isaiah*, 45; Sweeney, *Isaiah*, 78–79.

18. Childs, *Isaiah*, 19.

19. Sweeney, *Isaiah*, 78–79.

Command	Actions / Items of Worship	Yhwh's Comment
No longer bring (v. 13)	Worthless offerings (v. 13) Incense (v. 13)	An abomination to me (v. 13) I cannot endure (v. 13)
	New moon, Sabbath, and assemblies (v. 13) New moons and festivals (v. 14) Spread your hands (v. 15) Magnify your prayer (v. 15)	I hate (v. 14) I will not look (v. 15) I will not listen (v. 15)
Wash up (v. 16) Clean up (v. 16) Remove (v. 16)	Evil deeds (from my sight) (v. 16)	
Cease doing (v. 16) Learn to do (v. 17) Seek (v. 17) Care for (v. 17) Judge for (v. 17) Defend (v. 17)	Evil (v. 16) Good (v. 17) Justice (v. 17) Oppressed (v. 17) Orphan (v. 17) Widow (v. 17)	

Verse 14 ends with an example of parallelism: "They are over me as a burden // I am weary of carrying them." Verse 15 ends with a phrase ("your hands are full of blood") that does not fit into the parallel structure evident throughout the rest of the text.[20] For this reason, attempts to supply a second half verse to the end of v. 15 go back as far as 1QIsaᵃ, but, as has been noted above, such efforts are unnecessary.[21]

As does Amos 5:21–24, so also Isa 1:10–17 refers to the human senses that Yhwh uses in responding to the people's offerings: in v. 11 it is the sense of taste when Yhwh declares that he is sated with the animal sacrifices; his sense of sight is mentioned in vv. 12, 15 and 16, and his sense of hearing is suggested in v. 15.

20. Kaiser (*Isaiah 1–12*, 25) suggests that the inclusion of the phrase יְדֵיכֶם דָּמִים מָלֵאוּ, "your hands are full of blood" may be the reason for 1QIsaᵃ's inserted plus of אצבעותיכם בעאון, "your fingers with iniquity," in view of the parallelism found in the rest of the unit. See n. r above.

21. Wildberger, *Isaiah 1–12*, 36; Blenkinsopp, *Isaiah 1–39*, 180; Kaiser, *Isaiah 1–12*, 25.

The inclusion of ten imperatives in the text (see chart above) underscores the urgency of the situation.[22] The people must understand the extent of their errors immediately and resolve to improve so as to abate Yhwh's anger.

On the basis of the above observations, the text can be structured as follows:[23]

v. 10   Call to attention
vv. 11–15   Yhwh's rejection of people's worship (whole-burnt offerings, sacrifice, assemblies, and prayer)
vv. 16–17   Resolution proposed

AUTHENTICITY AND DATING

In the modern era Duhm was the first to identify the three major redactions of the book, dividing it into what are currently referred to as First, Second, and Third Isaiah.[24] In dividing the book thus, Duhm credits the eighth-century prophet with the primary text of its first 39 chapters.[25] Duhm's divisions are now the standard among scholars.[26] Dissenting theories include those of Oswalt and Motyer, who claim that the entire book of Isaiah is the product of the eighth-century BC prophet,[27] and Kaiser, who states about 1:10–17, "it derives from an anonymous prophetic writer of the early postexilic period working against the background of the second temple."[28] Kaiser bases his argument on the purportedly Deuteronomistic language found throughout the passage.[29] Blenkinsopp, however, concludes that Kaiser's argument

22. Oswalt (*Isaiah*, 94) understands the imperatives as "bitter words laden with sarcasm," although the tone seems more one of urgency.

23. For alternative structures, see Sweeney, *Isaiah*, 78–79; Motyer, *Isaiah*, 45; Oswalt, *Isaiah*, 61.

24. Duhm, *Jesaja*, 19.

25. Ibid.

26. Blenkinsopp, *Isaiah 1–39*, 184; Wildberger, *Isaiah 1–12*, 38; Sweeney, *Isaiah*, 41; Childs, *Isaiah*, 17; Seitz, *Isaiah*, 23.

27. Oswalt, *Isaiah*, 25–26; Motyer, *Isaiah*, 25.

28. Kaiser, *Isaiah 1–12*, 25.

29. Kaiser (*Isaiah 1–12*, 27–28) states, "The only parallel to the phrase 'seek something from someone's hand' which opens v.12b is in I Sam. 20.16 and thus in a Deuteronomistic

based on the text's Deuteronomistic language does not demonstrate its Deuteronomistic theology.[30] It is possible that terms now regarded as "Deuteronomistic" were current already in the eighth century, though the corresponding theology developed two centuries later as an outgrowth of the (post)exilic experience. The concepts used in this unit, such as Yhwh's refusal of various aspects of Israelite worship, are also spoken of by the other eighth-century BC biblical prophets, Amos, Hosea, and Micah.[31] Accordingly, I view the pericope as the work of the eighth-century prophet, Isaiah ben Amoz (1:1).[32]

The historical time period in which Isaiah prophesied is reflected in the passage with its mention of normal Temple activities: regular whole-burnt offerings, sacrifices, burning of incense, celebration of annual, monthly, and weekly festival days (vv. 11–15). Such regular worship observance indicates the peaceful situation of the country politically. Given that it presupposes that regular sacrifices, celebration of new moons, festival days, and normal worship service and prayer were occurring in the Temple, the most likely time period for 1:10–17 could be either following the incident with Ahaz (Isaiah 7–8), 732–714, or shortly prior to Sennacherib's threat, but after Isaiah's second round of prophetic activity, thus: about 710–702 BC.[33]

UNIT IN ITS CONTEXT

Scholars believe that chap. 1 may have originally existed as an independent collection of the eighth-century prophet's preaching.[34] The six individual units (1:2–3, 4–9, 10–17, 18–20, 21–26, 29–31) within the

---

text . . . the formula 'the evil of deeds' which we find in 16aβ hardly occurs at all in the eighth century, but is to be found rather in the later seventh and early sixth centuries; it is used frequently in the book of Jeremiah, including its Deuteronomistic strata...the demand to give their rights to the widow and the fatherless is one of the prominent features of the thought of Deuteronomic and Deuteronomistic theology."

30. Blenkinsopp (*Isaiah 1–39*, 181) points out that the language cited by Kaiser and used in the Isaiah text is conventional for the eighth century BC and "by no means confined to Deuteronom[ist]ic writings, so a verdict of not proven seems appropriate."

31. Cf. Amos 5:21–25; Hos 6:6; Mic 6:1–8.

32. Wildberger, *Isaiah 1–12*, 33–39; Blenkinsopp, *Isaiah 1–39*, 181; Childs, *Isaiah*, 17.

33. Blenkinsopp, *Isaiah 1–39*, 91; Sweeney, *Isaiah*, 80.

34. Wildberger, *Isaiah 1–12*, 9; Sweeney, *Isaiah*, 63.

chapter were gathered together to form a whole, although when and by whom this happened, remains a question.[35] Sweeney says the whole chapter exhibits a trial genre pattern with persuasive language featuring catchword connections.[36] Evidence of the trial genre is found in vv. 2–20 with an appeal for witnesses (vv. 2–3), a statement of the charge (vv. 4–9), an instruction concerning illicit and licit behavior (vv. 10–17), and an appeal to begin legal proceedings (vv. 18–20).[37] Another feature of the chapter that unifies it, Sweeney claims, is the focus on the need for the people to change established patterns of behavior.[38]

Sweeney further affirms that Isaiah is the speaker throughout the entire chapter, whose unifying feature is the requirement that the people change their behavior.[39] Sweeney's argument works in the sense that the individual passages combined in Isaiah 1 form a continuous message, and that all units have the prophet as speaker.[40] Seitz also sees chapter one as a single composition that summarizes Isaiah's vision as mentioned in 1:1.[41] He believes that the chapter provides a summary of the prophet's teaching from the perspective of the events of 701 BC.[42] Childs says the separate passages within the first chapter have taken on a new literary function that is distinct from their original role because they now function as an introduction to the entire book.[43] On a similar note, Oswalt, who conceives of the entire book of Isaiah as the work of the eighth-century prophet, explains chapters one to five as the introduction to the prophecy because Isaiah's call vision occurs only in

35. Wildberger, *Isaiah 1–12*, 9; Sweeney, *Isaiah*, 63.

36. Sweeney (*Isaiah*, 64) notes catchword connections between vv. 2–3 and 4–9 ("sons" and "corrupt sons"), and between vv. 4–9 and 10–17 (common mention of "Sodom and Gomorrah"). Verses 10–17 and 18–20 are linked by the reference in 15b to "hands full of blood" and in v. 18 to the "redness" of the people's sins. He further notes that both v. 17 ("seek justice") and v. 18 ("we shall arbitrate") use legal terminology in regard to repentance. Finally, he identifies a catchword *inclusio* that unites v. 2 ("for Yhwh has spoken") and v. 20 ("for the mouth of Yhwh has spoken").

37. Ibid., 64–65. Wildberger (*Isaiah 1–12*, 9) identifies vv. 2–3 as a judgment speech, vv. 4–9 as a reproach, and vv. 10–17 as the accusations Yhwh makes against the people.

38. Sweeney, *Isaiah*, 64.

39. Ibid., 63–64.

40. Ibid., 64.

41. Seitz, *Isaiah*, 23.

42. Ibid.

43. Childs, *Isaiah*, 16.

chapter six.[44] Motyer also identifies chapters one to five as a unit because of the absence of any distinguishing historical markers such as names or dates, but identifies three divisions (1:1–31; 2:1–4:6; 5:1–30) within these five chapters with a common focus on God's rebellious people.[45] Specifically, he further divides the first chapter into three scenes of "national calamity (vv. 6–8), religious declension (vv. 10–15), and social collapse (vv. 21–23) arising from rebellion (v. 2), misdemeanor (v. 15), and infidelity (v. 21)."[46]

Wildberger views 1:10–17 as one of six independent utterances that were joined together "to form an impressive unity."[47] Blenkinsopp sees a continuous rhetorical theme throughout the chapter that denounces first the whole people of Israel, then the religious and civil leaders, and finally Jerusalem for social injustices.[48] While both Wildberger and Blenkinsopp provide plausible arguments for unity within the chapter, it seems fruitless to attempt to explain how or why the redactors finally settled on the order in which the various oracles in chap. one now appear.

EXEGETICAL ANALYSIS

Yhwh's speech begins with questions concerning the multiple forms of public worship, sacrifices and whole-burnt offerings (vv. 11, 13). It proceeds with a denial of the validity of Temple pilgrimages (v. 12). It then denounces communal celebrations (vv. 13–14); and denies the efficacy of individual prayers (v. 15). Following the criticism, an element of hope is proffered by means of the suggestion that the people purify their lives (v. 16). The text ends with a divine lesson which states the specific conduct that Yhwh expects of his people (v. 17).

44. Oswalt, *Isaiah*, 60–61.
45. Motyer, *Isaiah*, 40–41.
46. Ibid.
47. Wildberger, *Isaiah 1–12*, 9.
48. Ibid., 180–8.

Verse 10

The call to attention in v. 10a, שִׁמְעוּ דְבַר־יְהוָה, "hear the word of Yhwh," appears in eighteen other places in the OT, ten of which are found in Jeremiah.[49] In v. 10b, immediately following the command to hear, one meets the phrase הַאֲזִינוּ תּוֹרַת אֱלֹהֵינוּ, "listen to the instruction of our God." This example of semantic parallelism that involves intensification ("hear" . . . "listen"; "the word of Yhwh" . . . "the instruction of our God") is a poetic device used in the prophetic literature to help the audience to remember and apply the message to their particular circumstances.[50] According to Jensen, this kind of call to attention is more characteristic of wisdom than of prophetic traditions.[51] Jensen says the combination of דְבַר־יְהוָה followed by תּוֹרַת אֱלֹהֵינוּ is "used to designate the instruction of the teacher within the wisdom tradition" to listen to the subsequent message.[52] The use of the "hear...listen" word-pair is unusual in the book of Isaiah, where it occurs only two other times as a means of evoking attention.[53]

The call to attention is not the only unusual feature in v.10. Isaiah compares the leaders to those who lived in Sodom and the people to those who lived in Gomorrah. This comparison would capture the attention of his audience and make clear that the misdeeds that follow are widespread throughout the land. There are other biblical passages

---

49. שִׁמְעוּ דְבַר־יְהוָה appears in the following verses: 2 Kgs 7:1; 2 Chr 18:18; Isa 8:14; 66:5; Jer 2:4; 7:2; 17:20; 19:3; 21:11; 29:20; 31:10; 42:15; 44:24, 26; Ezek 13:2; 34:9; 36:11; 37:4; and Hos 4:1. The phrase, slightly varied, שִׁמְעוּ דְבַר־אֲדֹנָי יהוה, appears also in Ezek 6:3; 25:3 and 36:4. Finally, the direct object marker is added to the phrase, שִׁמְעוּ אֶת־דְּבַר יְהוָה, in Ezek 34:7. The presence (or absence) of the direct object marker has no bearing on the translation.

50. Alter (*Biblical Poetry*, 19–21) identifies intensification as a feature of semantic parallelism, which can be "achieved by the introduction of a simile or metaphor in the second verset that brings out the full force of meaning of an image occurring in the first verset" (21). In Isa 1:10 the command to hear is intensified by the command to listen; the object "word of Yhwh" is similarly heightened in the second half, with its reference to *tôrâ* as the "instruction of our God."

51. Jensen, *Use of tôrâ*, 70. See also Job 13:17; 21:2; 34:2, 16; Ps 78:1; Prov 1:8; 4:1; 6:20.

52. Ibid., 71.

53. The only other time Isaiah uses this "Hear . . . listen" opening is in 1:2. He uses the phrase in the reverse order in 28:23, "Listen . . . hear."

which compare the people's behavior to that of Sodom and Gomorrah.[54] There are two in the book of Isaiah itself: in the immediately preceding 1:9b, and again in 3:9, where both Judah and Jerusalem are warned about their behavior via a comparison of the people to those who lived in Sodom. The comparison also occurs in Ezek 16:49, where Jerusalem is chastised for behaving worse than Sodom. Brueggemann states, "In poetic imagination the rulers and people of Jerusalem are identified and addressed as Sodom and Gomorrah instead of being contrasted with them. The beloved Holy City has been renamed by the most abhorrent name imaginable, the most despicable, deplorable name available."[55]

Jensen notes that this verse may be compared to teaching in the wisdom tradition, given its phrase תּוֹרַת אֱלֹהֵינוּ, "the instruction of our God."[56] The word תּוֹרָה occurs seven times in chaps. 1–39, each time referring to the "instruction" the people are supposed to be following, but have failed to do so.[57] In the next verse Isaiah begins to clarify which practices the people are following that are displeasing to Yhwh.

Verse 11

Isaiah is the speaker in v. 10, but in v. 11 Yhwh himself begins to address the Israelites. He first asks a question, then provides his own answer, albeit one that is contrary to anything the people had heretofore believed. Jensen notes that a call to attention followed by a rhetorical question is a common pattern in wisdom compositions.[58] Although the questioner does not expect an answer to such a question, Yhwh proceeds to give one. This change in speaker, from prophet to God, is unique in the book

---

54. Biblical passages that refer to the fate of Sodom and or Gomorrah in warning to their current audiences include Jer 23:14; 49:18; 50:40; Amos 4:11.

55. Brueggemann, *Isaiah*, 17.

56. Jensen, *Isaiah*, 45. Jensen says, "Those [Isaiah] addresses as *rulers* (*qesinim*) would probably have been among those who received the education and instruction designed for aspiring scribes and court officials, as well as for the sons of well-to-do families."

57. First Isaiah uses *tôrâ* here in 1:10, as well as in 2:3; 5:24; 8:16, 20; 24:5; 30:9. Second Isaiah uses it five times in 42:4, 21, 24; 51:4, 7; Third Isaiah never uses the term. Jensen (*Use of* tôrâ, 68–73) discusses the origins of *tôrâ* in wisdom traditions, but concludes that the change of speaker within 1:10 from the prophet's call to attention to Yhwh's instruction indicates a deviation from "simple wisdom composition" (p. 73).

58. Jensen (*Isaiah*, 45) notes that this pattern also occurs in Job 13:6; 21:2; 34:16; 37:14; Ps 49:2–6; Isa 28:23–24.

of Isaiah and reveals the depth of Yhwh's anger concerning the situation, for, to the best of my knowledge, nowhere else in the book does such a change in speaker occur. Yhwh here usurps the role of the prophet (to bring the message of Yhwh to the people), because the subject is so important to him. Given that Yhwh overrides the prophet and delivers the oracle "in person," the significance of the message becomes all the more important for the audience.

The rhetorical question posed here ("What are your many sacrifices to me?") demonstrates Yhwh's frustration with the people. Four other times in the OT Yhwh states that he does not appreciate the most important outward signs of the Temple cult.[59] Following the question in 11b, Yhwh begins to list the offerings he abhors: whole-burnt offerings, rams, fatlings, and the blood of bulls, lambs and goats. As Brueggemann says, "All were heretofore accepted, legitimated offerings; all are now flatly rejected."[60] Jensen also points out the order and progression of what is being rejected, "for the listing goes from the external rites (sacrifices, food offerings, incense – vv. 11–13a) to the less tangible matters of feasts and assemblies (vv. 13b–14) to prayer itself (v. 15)."[61] Also of note is the progression within Yhwh's rejection itself. In v. 11 he states שָׂבַעְתִּי, "I am sated," and לֹא חָפָצְתִּי, "I am not pleased"; his displeasure increases in v. 13 to לֹא־אוּכַל, "I cannot endure," and culminates in v. 14 with, שָׂנְאָה נַפְשִׁי, "I hate to my soul."

In Isaiah's time, sacrifices in the southern kingdom were offered in the Temple in Jerusalem.[62] By postexilic times sacrifices were performed every day, morning and evening, as an offering to God.[63] Such activity would have had its roots in preexilic Israelite worship, although

---

59. Amos 5:21 ("I hate, I reject your feasts, nor will I even take delight in your solemn assemblies"); Jer 6:20 ("Of what use to me incense that comes from Sheba, or sweet cane from far-off lands? Your whole-burnt offerings find no favor with me, your sacrifices please me not"); Ps 50:8 ("Not for your sacrifices do I rebuke you, nor for your whole-burnt offerings, set before me daily"); and Mal 1:10 ("Oh, that one among you would shut the temple gates to keep you from kindling fire on my altar in vain! I have no pleasure in you, says Yhwh of hosts; neither will I accept any sacrifice from your hands").

60. Brueggemann, *Isaiah*, 17.

61. Jensen, *Isaiah*, 45.

62. Although their composition postdates Isaiah, see 1 Kgs 9:1–3 and 2 Chr 11:13–17. The Temple in Jerusalem is the only temple in the Southern Kingdom mentioned in the Bible.

63. Exod 29:38–39.

there is nothing in the biblical text that specifies the quantity or quality of preexilic sacrifice. Accordingly, the tone and content of v. 11 may well have shocked the people, above all since Yhwh himself delivers the message. The message seems to contradict the cultic customs that had developed since the construction of the Temple.[64] The system of sacrifices was established and in "good working order."[65] Clearly, people would have thought, Yhwh could not but be pleased with their coming to the Temple to worship![66] Nonetheless, the accusations continue into the next verse, for the sacrifices are not the only things that Yhwh views as abhorrent.

Verse 12

מִיֶּדְכֶם is literally rendered: "from your hands." The LXX is clearer regarding the problem by locating the trampling specifically in, τὴν αὐλήν μου, "my courtyard."[67] Solomon's Temple, the one with which Isaiah was familiar, consisted of three areas: the inner-most section was the דְּבִיר, the "Holy of Holies," where the ark of the covenant was kept (1 Kgs 6:19). This space measured twenty cubits square (1 Kgs 6:2, 17). Outside of this area was the הֵיכָל, the "Holy Place," wherein the מִזְבֵּחַ, "altar," was located (1 Kgs 6:22).[68] Finally, outside the two aforementioned areas,

---

64. Wildberger (*Isaiah 1–12*, 41) notes: "One cannot easily determine which specific notions were held by Isaiah's contemporaries when they thought of sacrifice, since, no doubt, there was no single, generally accepted viewpoint concerning sacrifice. The use of זבח (sacrifice) and עלה (burnt offering), without distinguishing them more specifically, shows that the original concepts which lie behind each of these terms had by and large lost their distinctive aspects. Wherever there is a critical assessment of sacrifice, both of these types of offerings always fall under the same verdict."

65. Blenkinsopp, *Isaiah 1–39*, 184.

66. It was not until later, when the written Torah was available to the people, that sixty-six verses in Exodus, Leviticus and Numbers specifically link sacrifices and offerings with atonement, but this is not to suggest that atonement is a solely postexilic idea that was attached to sacrificial activities in the Temple. The fat and certain organs of the sacrifice were burnt to produce a "pleasing odor" (Lev 3:3–5) and the blood was sprinkled on the altar (Lev 5:9), acts that were meant to atone for sin (Lev 4:20b). Each of the sacrifices and offerings was intended to provide a sense of at-one-ment with God (Leviticus 1–7, 28–29).

67. See n. i above.

68. The altar in the sanctuary is the golden altar for burning incense mentioned in 1 Kgs 6:22. It is not until the postexilic composition of 1 Chr 6:34 that the two altars are explicitly distinguished: עַל־מִזְבַּח הָעוֹלָה וְעַל־מִזְבַּח הַקְּטֹרֶת, "the altar of whole-burnt offerings

was the אֻלָם, "porch" that measured twenty cubits wide by ten cubits deep (1 Kgs 6:3), and this אֻלָם was flanked by a pair of columns named יָכִין, "Jachin," and בֹּעַז, "Boaz" (1 Kgs 7:21).[69] Whole-burnt offerings were burnt on another מִזְבֵּחַ that was in front of the אֻלָם (2 Kgs 16:14).[70] The description in 1 Kings includes details of הֶחָצֵר הַפְּנִימִית, "the inner court" (6:3) and 1 Kgs 7:12 distinguishes between the וְלַחֲצַר בֵּית־יהוה הַפְּנִימִית, "inner court of the temple of Yhwh" and the לְאֻלָם הַבָּיִת, "temple porch." The reference to a court conforms to the term Isaiah uses in v. 12, i.e., חָצֵר, "court." In v. 12, חָצֵר appears in the plural construct with the first person common singular pronoun suffix, and is translated "my courts." It is unclear whether the two terms חָצֵר and אֻלָם refer to the same type of structure, i.e., if a porch and a court are the same thing.[71] The area called the חָצֵר was where people came to present their offerings to the priests for sacrifice, thus walking on, or "trampling," Yhwh's court.

The people were required to appear before Yhwh on specified days each year. Exod 23:17 states: "Three times each year all males will appear before the Lord, Yhwh." They are not being criticized by Yhwh here

---

and the altar of incense"; although see 1 Kgs 6:20–22; 9:25.

69. *HALOT*, 1. 41, says that אֻלָם is an architectural technical term, referring to the "porch" of a palace or temple. See also Meyers, "Temple," 6. 357 for the position of the pillars.

70. 1 Kings 8. Meyers ("Temple," 359) states: "The explanation for this omission perhaps lies in the role of Solomon's predecessor in the temple project. David had already built an altar at the place he had chosen for the Temple and had proceeded to offer sacrifices there (2 Sam 24:21, 25; cf. 1 Chr 21:18–22:1), thus initiating the altar and, in a sense, temple sacrifice long before Solomon's dedicatory feast."

71. It is possible that the use of both terms, חָצֵר and אֻלָם, demonstrates redactions of the books of Kings. חָצֵר is used 191 times throughout the OT in 164 verses. In 1 Kings it is used six times; twice to refer to part of Solomon's palace (1 Kgs 7:8, 12a) and four times to refer to part of the Temple (1 Kgs 6:36; 7:9, 12b; 8:64). It is used in the description of the Tent of Meeting thirty-six times (i.e., see Exodus 27, 35, 38) and as part of the Temple, whether the inner or outer court, eighty-two times (a short list includes 2 Kgs 20:4; 21:5; 23:12; 2 Chr 4:9; 7:7; Pss 65:5; 84:3; 96:8; Jer 19:14; 26:2; Ezek 40:17; 42:3; and Zech 3:7). Other uses of חָצֵר include references to guard houses (twelve times; see Jeremiah 32), courtyards in private homes or palaces (twelve times; see 2 Sam 17:18; Neh 8:16; Esth 1:5), and to villages (forty-nine times; see Gen 25:16; Lev 25:31; Josh 13:28; 15:41; 18:28). By contrast, אֻלָם is used sixty-one times in forty-one verses. This term appears seven times in 1 Kings (6:3; 7:6, 7, 8, 12, 19, 21), once in 1 Chronicles (28:11), five times in 2 Chronicles (3:4; 8:12; 15:8; 29:7, 17), forty-seven times in Ezekiel (see, i.e., 8:16; 40:7, 21, 36; 41:15; 46:8), and once in the book of Joel (2:17). I suggest that אֻלָם is a Late Hebrew term introduced to the language after the time of Isaiah.

for coming to fulfill that duty, but rather for "trampling" the courts.[72] The use of the term רְמֹס in v. 12, although no destruction is involved, suggests that the people are milling around, as do mindless animals. The next verse will make clear why Yhwh considers their required appearance before him little different from a stampede.

Verse 13

Yhwh has become fatigued with the people who bring offerings since they are not coming with the proper attitude that he expects. In v. 11 Yhwh finds no pleasure in the plethora of animals brought into the Temple as offerings. The people are not at one with their God; he deems their insincerity an outrage. The incense they offer, via the priests, is rejected; their celebration of the feasts has been performed with the wrong attitude. Childs speaks of the mass of worshippers piling into the Temple "to fulfill their sacrificial obligations as well as the appointed sacral feasts."[73] He says they are merging obligations and feasts, "riding roughshod over careful priestly protocol," so that Isaiah rejects them all as scandalous in the eyes of the "very God whom they believed had called for these forms of worship."[74] I disagree with Childs because the text indicates that the people in fact carried out the priestly protocol diligently; it is for another reason that Yhwh indicts the priests and the people (see vv. 15–16). Yhwh continues the accusations into the next verse, explaining how the people's cultic actions affect him.

Verse 14

Yhwh continues the diatribe against the people for practices performed by them with an unacceptable disposition. He also explains the effect that all of their behavior has on him: it weighs him down; it is too heavy to bear. All their empty activities thoroughly repulse him. He is entirely sickened, not by "Israel's carefully orchestrated rituals," as Childs

---

72. "Trampling" is one of Isaiah's favorite terms for describing the damage caused by repeated and/or heavy treading. First Isaiah uses the root רמס, in addition to this verse, in 5:5; 7:25; 10:6; 16:4; and 28:18, each time to describe something as rendered unusable for its intended purpose.

73. Childs, *Isaiah*, 19.

74. Ibid.

claims,[75] but rather by Israel's hypocrisy and attempts to manipulate God. There is another occasion on which Isaiah speaks against someone's empty performance. He will tell Ahaz that his refusal to make a request of Yhwh has tried God's patience and he is left fatigued by the king's insincere farce.[76] Brueggemann states of Isa 1:14, "Yahweh rejects them because Israel's gestures of worship are no longer vehicles for a serious relationship."[77] By this point, Yhwh has rejected every public form of worship; in the next verse he will move to a more personal religious form: prayer itself.

Verse 15

The text continues to articulate the outrage Yhwh feels when confronted by the charade of false worship, now including even the prayers offered by the people. The text explains why God has chosen to stop listening: the people offer sacrifices with "bloody" hands. The euphemism, the people's hands are not literally bloody, indicates the level of hypocrisy that the people manifest when they offer sacrifices, appear before Yhwh, and pray.[78] The blood that covers their outstretched hands is a result of the violence done against the helpless members of society.[79]

The gesture of spreading out one's hands in prayer is also mentioned in 1 Kgs 8:22 when Solomon does this before the altar of Yhwh, as well as in Lam 1:17 when Zion stretches out her hands in prayer but there is no one who hears her. Isaiah 8:17 observes that Yhwh is not listening

75. Ibid.

76. Isa 7:13.

77. Brueggemann, *Isaiah,* 17.

78. Andersen and Freedman (*Micah,* 353–55, 382–83) note a similar accusation by Micah, one of Isaiah's contemporaries, against those who consume cooked human flesh (Micah 3:3) and build Jerusalem in blood (3:10)—perhaps a reference to using human sacrifices in building foundations (a practice common to Israel's neighbors) (382–83). For further references to "bloody hands" that also seem to refer to general violence resulting in human bloodshed, see Ezek 23:37, 45; Isa 59:3. Additional accusations of bloodshed involving violence against other people in the community appear in Ezek 22:13, 25–28; Jer 22:3. In short, the people are participating in violence against one another, yet they also go to the Temple to perform their religious duties and for this Yhwh rejects even their prayer (Isa 1:15).

79. Wildberger (*Isaiah 1–12,* 48) points out that the hands are extended outward and upward to enable the god to fill them, as in "Vergil's *Aeneid* 1.93: *duplicis tendens ad sidera palmas* (stretching out both of the palms to the skies)."

to the prayers of the people; here, too, it is because of the sins of the people.[80] The accusation is clear: the people have presented themselves to pray before the Lord without making the proper preparations, such as a change of behavior towards those in society who require assistance.

After this long list of offenses, Yhwh finally offers hope that the people will once again be enabled to offer acceptable sacrifices. Via this indication about how they can rectify the situation, the reason why their worship and sacrifice was unacceptable becomes clear.

Verse 16

The commands to wash and be clean in this verse are peculiar in the context of an address to people who have entered the Temple intent on worship and sacrifice. There were many rituals to ensure that the people were ritually clean and thus fit to appear in the Temple.[81] The addressees should then have already cleaned themselves, lest they defile the Temple. The rest of the verse explains why Yhwh deems them nevertheless still unclean: they have performed evil deeds and have chosen wickedness. Yhwh rejected their sacrifices because the people were going through the motions as instructed, but had not internalized the instruction. They were physically clean on the outside, but inside they were not. To Yhwh, the people's internal uncleanness was manifested externally through the evil deeds they did when they were no longer taking part in the Temple worship services.

The phrase used by the prophet here, רֹעַ מַעַלְלֵיכֶם, appears four other times in the OT, all in the book of Jeremiah. Wildberger explains that Jeremiah "used [the phrase] in admonitions and in announcements of judgment."[82] The people have done so many malevolent deeds they no longer recognize that what they are doing is evil. While מַעֲלָל can refer to any deed, whether good or evil, "Isaiah always uses it in a negative sense."[83] Wildberger suggests that, for Isaiah, a מַעֲלָל is a "crime," as opposed to a simple malevolent action.

---

80. The phrase is repeated in Isa 59:3.

81. Scattered throughout the (later) book of Leviticus are numerous instructions concerning various ways to make oneself ritually clean and, therefore, to be able to enter the presence of Yhwh. See especially Leviticus 11–16.

82. Wildberger, *Isaiah 1–12*, 49. The references are Jer 4:4; 21:12; 23:2; and 44:22.

83. Wildberger, *Isaiah 1–12*, 49. See Isa 3:8, 10.

To this point in the oracle it is still unclear which of the people's evil deeds have caught Yhwh's attention. In the next verse he will state precisely what is wrong, and how they may once again gain his favor.

Verse 17

Finally the problem is clear: the people have set wrong priorities in their Temple worship, to the exclusion, or to the detriment of the disadvantaged in their midst. The concept that Isaiah highlights here in v. 17 of providing equal treatment to all members of Israelite society is also addressed in the Torah, in Deut 1:17, which declares that the people must give equal and appropriate attention to the small and great members of society alike.[84] Leviticus 19:15 is just as clear a command, "You shall do no injustice in judgment. Show neither partiality to the poor nor honor to the great, but judge your fellow in righteousness." That the books of Deuteronomy and Leviticus, both of which were composed sometime after Isaiah, include written instructions that pick up on Isaiah's teaching demonstrates that the illicit activities of the eighth-century Israelites denounced by Isaiah perdured and had to be addressed again in succeeding generations.

Also in connection with Isa 1:17, Jensen directs attention to the wisdom tradition, in which the leaders of the people were trained, that specifically taught them to pay close attention to the poor and helpless members of society, to ensure that the needs of all members would be addressed.[85] In spite of all the ritual activities the leaders and the people performed on a regular basis, they were ignoring the needs of their neighbors. The practice of their religion was out of focus and the people needed a corrective lens to clearly envision the scene as Yhwh viewed it so that their future ritual activity could be performed in acceptable fashion.

---

84. See also Deut 16:19.

85. Jensen, *Isaiah*, 46, "Cf. Prov 14:31; 15:25; 19:17; 22:9; 22:22–23; 23:10–11; 29:14." Additionally, see Pss 35:10; 68:5; 72:4; 140:12; 146:9; and Job 31:16; and from the prophetic literature: Jer 22:3; Zech 7:10; Mal 3:5.

SUMMARY

The book of Isaiah begins with a series of oracles intended to draw the people's attention to a situation that was deemed unacceptable by Yhwh. Isa 1:10–17 cites Yhwh's rejection of the various Temple rituals that were so familiar to the people. The oracle features a series of direct accusations by Yhwh himself, indicating that every familiar form of worship is rejected by him, one by one, until the reader is left asking what the people can do to return to the right path to acceptable communication with their God. Worship, in and of itself, is not what is rejected. It was rather the attitudes and the behaviors of the people toward their neighbors who were in need with which Yhwh finds fault. Isaiah's purpose here, via an oracle intended to shock the people into paying attention, is to redirect the people back to the proper mind-set and conduct so that they would be in right relationship with each other and with their God.

During the first half of the eighth century BC, the kingdoms of Israel and Judah were relatively peaceful, affluent, and comfortable. City life was calm, priests oversaw the religious activities in the temples, and Assyrian threats were muted. As is wont to happen, with calm and comfort came a relaxation of the rules, because the collective memory of humans is short-lived. As soon as life began to look good and military threats receded, and, once people grew comfortable with the way things were, they began to place more value on comfort, the calm, the relaxation, and forgot to give credit to the source of this condition. The associated smug attitudes with which the people treated each other, their worship and their God brought their relationship with Yhwh into serious jeopardy. In their attempts to rush to the Temple to offer sacrifices to celebrate their blessings, they were ignoring the needs of their fellow Israelites who could not care for themselves. The principle means of communication with God was seen to consist in the activities that took place in the Temple. In time, the people began to take advantage of the rituals, by abusing the rites, by neglecting their less advantaged neighbors, and thus devaluing their offerings.

Beginning in 745, with the rise of the Assyrian king, Tiglath-Pileser III, this period of Israelite calm began to erode as the continual foreign military threat took its toll. This admonition was intended to warn the people that their behavior was disrespectful of each other and of their God. Isaiah tried to teach the people that their problems stemmed from a series of misguided priorities. He made a connection between the people's obligation of social justice toward their neighbors and their obligation to worship Yhwh. The people's priorities were out of balance, and it became the task of this prophet to draw their attention to what should have been the higher priority for them. Isaiah undertook to help the people see that while their worship was not wrong, in and of itself, it was not as necessary as taking care of the needs of their neighbors. The prophet observed that the temple activities had become the people's only form of worship. The internalization of their relationship with Yhwh that should have been strengthened by their Temple participation was neglected. The blessings the people sought were withheld because their outward behaviors did not express any sense of concern for others. Isaiah sought to teach the people that by caring for each other the Israelites showed true worship of Yhwh, and it was only after everyone was cared for in a respectful manner, that sacrifices might acceptably be offered. Yhwh's priority was the care of his people. God's intention, through the voice of his prophet, was to make this his people's priority as well. The people had to love their neighbors in order to love Yhwh.

5

Comparing and Contrasting Amos and Isaiah

IN THIS BOOK I have undertaken an extensive study of Amos 5:21–24 and Isa 1:10–17 within their historical and literary contexts. I have especially sought to focus on similar language and content, historical background, and use of sources by either Amos or Isaiah or both of them in their criticism of the cult in Israel and Judah. A thorough investigation of these texts is important to better understand the messages of the prophets and how these messages can contribute to an appreciation of the phenomenon of prophetic criticism of the preexilic cult. In this chapter I will begin by presenting a comparison of the two texts that have been the focus of this work, then by noting the differences between them. On this basis, I will then summarize my findings.

COMPARISON OF TEXT OF AMOS 5:21–24 AND ISAIAH 1:10–17

In an attempt to compare the two oracles, scholars have noted similarities in the vocabulary utilized in Amos 5:21–23 and Isa 1:11–16, that is, in each prophet's accusation against the people.[1] The following chart

---

1. Paul, *Amos*, 189; Wolff, *Joel and Amos*, 262–63; Wildberger, *Isaiah 1–12*, 35, 42, 46; Blenkinsopp, *Isaiah 1–39*, 181.

may clarify the terms common in the two oracles. The Hebrew term from *BHS* is followed by my own translation.

Amos 5:21	שָׂנֵאתִי	"I hate"	Isaiah 1:14	שָׂנְאָה	"I hate"
	עַצְּרֹתֵיכֶם	"your solemn assemblies"	1:13	עֲצָרָה	"assembly"
v. 22	עֹלוֹת	"whole-burnt offerings"	1:11	עֹלוֹת	"whole-burnt offerings"
	וּמִנְחֹתֵיכֶם	"your grain offerings"	1:13	מִנְחַת	"grain offerings"
	מְרִיאֵיכֶם	"your fatted animals"	1:11	מְרִיאִים	"fatted animals"
v. 23	הָסֵר מֵעָלַי	"remove from me"	1:16	הָסִירוּ ... מִנֶּגֶד עֵינָי	"remove ... from my sight"
	לֹא אֶשְׁמָע	"I will not listen"	1:15	אֵינֶנִּי שֹׁמֵעַ	"I will not listen"

In addition, there are instances where the same concept occurs in both oracles, although not in identical words. The following chart illustrates these similarities.

Amos 5:21	חַגֵּיכֶם	"your feasts"	1:14	חָדְשֵׁיכֶם וּמוֹעֲדֵיכֶם	"your new moons and your annual festivals"
v. 22	לֹא אַבִּיט	"I will not look upon"	1:15	אַעְלִים עֵינַי	"I close my eyes"
	לֹא אֶרְצֶה	"I will not accept"	1:11	לֹא חָפַצְתִּי	"I am not pleased"

In noting the foregoing similar terms and ideas, scholars have discussed the possibility that one prophet was used as a source by the other, and generally conclude that Amos's text was available to Isaiah.[2] Fey compares parallel blocks of prophetic material, including Amos 5:21–25 and Isa 1:10–17, and determines that Isaiah had access to at least one-third of the current text of Amos when he composed his own material.[3] Given the dating of Amos's oracles (760–745) and Isaiah's three periods of ministry (740–701), Fey's suggestion is plausible. No scholar has proposed a pre-existing source for Amos's oracle of 5:21–24,

2. Blenkinsopp, *Isaiah 1–39*, 181; Childs, *Isaiah*, 19; Ernst, *Kultkritik*, 163–9; Fey (*Amos und Jesaja*, 144–7) concludes that Isaiah used Amos as a source for 1:10–17, although Isaiah formulates the message in his own terms.

3. Fey, *Amos und Jesaja*, 144.

although, as was established in Chapter 2, there are certainly influences from Wisdom traditions reflected in his book. The similarity between the two texts in theme and content cannot be denied. Certainly, the possibility exists that Amos prophesied first and his message was repeated and recalled throughout Israel and Judah, and that Isaiah subsequently delivered a similar message. I will, however, reserve my judgment on the matter until after I contrast the two passages.

DIFFERENCES IN TEXT OF AMOS 5:21–24 AND ISAIAH 1:10–17

There are a considerable number of differences between the two passages, Amos 5:21–24 and Isa 1:10–17. Looking at the two messages as a whole, the first obvious difference is that Isaiah's prophecy is twice as long as that of Amos, i.e., eight verses as opposed to four.[4] Secondly, the message of Amos proceeds in the following sequence: חַגֵּיכֶם, "your feasts" (v. 21), עַצְּרֹתֵיכֶם, "your solemn assemblies" (v. 21), עֹלוֹת וּמִנְחֹתֵיכֶם, "whole-burnt offerings and your grain offerings" (v.22), שֶׁלֶם מְרִיאֵיכֶם, "peace offerings of your fatted animals" (v. 22), הֲמוֹן שִׁרֶיךָ, "your noisy songs" (v. 23), and זִמְרַת נְבָלֶיךָ, "melody of your lyres" (v.23). By contrast, Isaiah orders the component items differently: עֹלוֹת, "whole-burnt offerings" (v. 11), כִּי תָבֹאוּ לֵרָאוֹת פָּנָי, Temple appearances (v.12), מִנְחַת, "grain offerings" (v. 13), קְטֹרֶת, "incense" (v. 13), חֹדֶשׁ וְשַׁבָּת, monthly feasts ("new moon"; repeated in v. 14) "and Sabbaths" (v. 13), קְרֹא מִקְרָא, "calling of assembly" (v. 13), וּמוֹעֲדֵיכֶם, "annual festivals" (v. 14), and תְּפִלָּה, "prayer" (v. 15). A third difference is that Amos's more "abstract" proposed resolution to the problems raised in vv. 21–23 is to let justice and righteousness flow like water in the community, whereas Isaiah spells out concretely what seeking justice entails: לִמְדוּ הֵיטֵב דִּרְשׁוּ מִשְׁפָּט אַשְּׁרוּ חָמוֹץ שִׁפְטוּ יָתוֹם רִיבוּ אַלְמָנָה, "learn to do good, seek justice, care for the oppressed, judge for the orphan, defend the widow" (v. 17). Amos 5:22 informs us that Yhwh will not look upon the peace offerings, but Isa 1:15 claims that Yhwh will not look at the people (lit., at you). Amos refers to וְזִמְרַת נְבָלֶיךָ הֲמוֹן שִׁרֶיךָ, loud songs and music, but Isaiah speaks of loud or much praying (תַרְבּוּ תְפִלָּה). Amos does not report the effect that all of the people's

---

4. This presupposes judgment on the secondary character of Amos 5:22aα, 25–27, as was discussed in chap. three.

actions has on Yhwh, while Isaiah makes this very clear: הָיוּ עָלַי לָטֹרַח נִלְאֵיתִי נְשֹׂא, "they are over me as a burden, and I am weary of carrying them" (1:14b). Amos mentions feasts and solemn assemblies (v. 21), but Isaiah names the celebrations of the new moon, the Sabbath, and the annual festivals (vv. 13–14). Finally, Amos's passage contains only one imperative, הָסֵר, "remove" (v. 23), while Isaiah's reading virtually explodes with demands: רַחֲצוּ, "Wash!," הִזַּכּוּ, "Clean!," הָסִירוּ, "Remove!," חִדְלוּ, "Cease!," לִמְדוּ, "Learn!," דִּרְשׁוּ, "Seek!," אַשְּׁרוּ, "Care for!," שִׁפְטוּ, "Judge for!," רִיבוּ, "Defend!" (vv. 16–17). Finally, there is no call to attention in the Amos reading, but Isaiah begins his prophecy with one (1:10). This plethora of differences leads to the conclusion that Fey is likely correct in his assertion that Isaiah knew of Amos's message at Bethel, but nevertheless took care to make the prophecy his own when he proclaims it in Jerusalem.

SUMMARY OF FINDINGS

Preexilic prophetic criticism of the cult has been viewed in modern times as an appeal to abolish the cult or as a plea for social justice within the community. However, the thirty-two Old Testament texts that criticize the praxis of the cult focus on idol worship, illicit offerings, accusations of corruption, or suggest alternate behaviors that would better align the Israelites with their God and with each other. Preexilic prophetic criticism of the cult, then, had in view neither an elimination of the cult nor merely a sympathetic care toward the widow, the orphan, and the oppressed. The feature shared by each of the Old Testament passages that contain criticism of the cult is a focus on the lack of proper attitude towards and respect for the relationship between the Israelite people and their God. What is above all required by Yhwh is doing justice and righteousness.

In my first chapter, I identified two similar texts of criticism of the cult, specifically Amos 5:21–24 and Isa 1:10–17, as the major focus for this present study. I then enumerated and discussed major scholarly proposals on such topics as explicit events that precipitated the specific prophetic criticism regarding cultic practices, how the praxis of the cult failed to include God, how the problems that the prophets criticized were not simply a matter of cult validity or social justice, and what could explain the sudden appearance on the scene of prophets who reject common practice in the temples.

In my second chapter, my first major task was to identify the social and economic structures of the eighth-century Israelite society, and what outside influences were manifested in the secular and religious realms of that society. I found that the Canaanites, who lived near the Israelites, did influence the political and economic systems adopted by the Israelite kingdoms. The Canaanite cult and the Israelite temple worship was investigated, and I determined that the Israelites always maintained that Yhwh was the sole recipient of their cultic worship. Similarly, the emergence of the Assyrians as a growing political threat provided the prophets with an urgent threat, ultimately emanating from Yhwh, should the Israelites not heed their warnings. The period of relative political calm in the mid- to late eighth century coincided with a lax attitude by those who participated in the temple cult. There followed a steady decline in justice and right behavior towards their neighbors, yet there was no noticeable change in the number of sacrifices offered in the temples. Such a situation led the prophets to speak against the cult in Israel and Judah.

In my third chapter, I treat Amos 5:21–24 as a mid-eighth-century composition that was most likely written by the prophet Amos himself. The passage fits into the wider context of the book of Amos as a critique of the Israelite's lack of justice within its own community. Amos addresses Israel's neighboring countries with oracles that threaten impending punishment. These oracles against the foreign nations begin Amos's overall lesson that Yhwh is the God of all people and can control the destiny of all people, not just the Israelites. When Amos turns his attention to the behaviors of the Israelites that have drawn Yhwh's wrath, he uses sarcasm to target specific behaviors and people as the objects of his criticism before he finally focuses in on cultic activities that were being carried out in the shrines and temples. His criticism of the cult elicits strong and swift reaction by the priest of Bethel, who has Amos ejected from that temple (Amos 7:12–13).

The text of Amos 5:21–23 lists elements of the cult that are henceforth to cease unless and until justice and righteousness (v. 24) permeate all facets of society, much like flowing water fills a streambed. The use of water similes in v. 24 highlights the degree to which justice and righteousness must flow throughout the community, never drying up if the community is to survive. Justice and righteousness in the lives of the Israelites, kindness toward their neighbors, right judgments at the city gates, proper weights and measures in the markets—these ways of worshipping Yhwh were far more important than offering an un-needed sacrifice.

As I note in my fourth chapter, Isa 1:10–17 is a later eighth-century composition that shares a number of similarities with Amos 5:21–24 and was composed by the author of First Isaiah. Isaiah ob-served in Jerusalem some of the same problems regarding the cult that Amos noted in Israel. Because the eighth-century Israelites from both Israel and Judah were abusing their neighbors, Yhwh spoke through the two prophets, one in each kingdom, to warn the people who came to worship in the temples that the external practice of the cult would be considered illicit until they internalized the behaviors of solicitude that had been a fundamental facet of their faith. If their injustices con-tinued, then Yhwh would send an enemy to take the people into exile. The Israelites would have to realize that Yhwh is God of the whole world, including their enemies.

The text of Isa 1:10–15, like Amos 5:21–23, lists facets of the cult that Yhwh rejects, but that had hitherto been considered necessary and good. Isaiah 1:17 explains the behaviors that are preferred by Yhwh, and, like Amos 5:24, declares that justice should be sought. Isaiah calls for the people to learn to do good and seek justice. These are aspects of Israelite life that needed greater attention than do celebrations and sac-rifices. The phrases that round off v. 17, "restore the oppressed," "judge for the orphan," and "defend the widow," explain how the people of Jerusalem could accomplish the verse's opening call to learn to do good and to seek justice. If the people treat the oppressed, the orphans, and the widows with justice, they will be acting well. If they return to treat-ing all members of their society with due consideration for traditionally exploited members, this is all Yhwh desires of the people.

The considerable amount of similar vocabulary in Amos 5:21–24 and Isa 1:10–17, as well as the variance in their time of composition, sug-gests the availability of one of these texts as the source for the other. As has been shown, Amos 5:21–24 was composed sometime between 760 and 745 BC, while Isa 1:10–17 was formulated sometime between 740 and 701 BC. Although Isaiah does not quote Amos's text, the likelihood is that he was aware of the older oracle and drew on its message when he composed his own. Scholars have yet to identify any pre-existing source for Amos's oracle, and conclude that his message was original.

In conclusion, I return to one of my original questions concerning the origin of the criticism of the cult at a certain period in Israelite history, namely, the eighth century BC. The problems that existed in Israelite culture occurred in both the northern and southern kingdoms; hence a prophet was sent to each community. The problems, as addressed in these two oracles, had nothing to do with the buildings, the temples or shrines, but with the actions of the people. The cultic actions were being rejected as long as the people did not correct their social interactions within the community. The economic and political life of the people was reflected in their temple worship in that those who could afford to offer sacrifices did so. These same people would have participated in the other activities that usually took place in the temple, such as singing of psalms, praying, and bringing offerings. However, the secular society, the life lived outside of temple activities, should also have reflected the same reverence for Yhwh as was being shown inside the temple. The festival celebrations were meant to be celebrated by all in the society, and this shared celebration should have reflected a society who cared for even its weakest members. Israelite justice demanded that all in the community be afforded equal treatment in matters of law, commerce, and religion. Righteousness would only be measured in terms of how the most unfortunate people in the society were being included in fair court decisions, equitable market transactions, and tolerable living conditions for all. Unless and until all received just and righteous treatment as a first priority, Yhwh would consider the praxis of the cult as unacceptable and undesirable.

It is my hope that the present study on Amos's and Isaiah's criticism of the cult has succeeded in shedding some light on one aspect of preexilic criticism of the cult. In light of my identification of the overall lack of justice and righteousness in both the northern and southern Israelite kingdoms in the eighth century, the seventh- and sixth-century biblical texts that contain cultic criticism might be more effectively studied.[5]

5. See chap. 1, pp. 3–4.

Further study of the cult in the northern kingdom as it developed apart from and in opposition to the accepted cult in the Temple in Jerusalem[6] may reveal additional problems regarded as illicit by the preexilic prophets. The prophetic critique concerning the temples and shrines in the northern kingdom as compared with that of the authors of the books of Kings would be an intriguing further topic of study.

6. See especially 1 Kgs 12:28–30; 13:33–34.

Bibliography

Abegg, Martin, Peter Flint and Eugene Ulrich, editors. *The Dead Sea Scrolls Bible: The Oldest Known Bible.* San Francisco: Harper, 1999.

Abusch, Tzvi. "Blood in Israel and Mesopotamia," in *Emanuel: Studies in Hebrew Bible, Septuagint, and Dead Sea Scrolls in Honor of Emanuel Tov,* edited by Shalom M. Paul, Robert A. Kraft, Lawrence H. Schiffman, and Weston W. Fields, 675–84. VTSup 94. Boston: Brill, 2003.

Ackerman, Susan. "Amos 5:18–24." *Interpretation* 57 (2003) 190–93.

Ah'ituv, Shmuel. "Land and Justice." In *Justice and Righteousness: Biblical Themes and Their Influence,* edited by Henning Graf Reventlow and Yair Hoffman, 11–28. JSOTSup 137. Sheffield: Sheffield University Press, 1992.

Albertz, Rainer. *A History of Israelite Religion in the Old Testament Period,* Vol. 1: *From the Beginnings to the End of the Monarchy.* Translated by John Bowden. OTL. Louisville: Westminster John Knox, 1994.

Alter, Robert. *The Art of Biblical Poetry.* New York: Basic Books, 1985.

Amit, Yairah. "The Jubilee Law—An Attempt at Instituting Social Justice." In *Justice and Righteousness: Biblical Themes and Their Influence,* edited by Henning Graf Reventlow and Yair Hoffman, 47–59. JSOTSup 137. Sheffield: Sheffield University Press, 1992.

Andersen, Francis I., and David Noel Freedman. *Amos: A New Translation with Introduction and Commentary.* AB 24A. New York: Doubleday, 1989.

———. *Micah: A New Translation with Introduction and Commentary.* AB 24E. New York: Doubleday, 2000.

Auld, A. G. *Amos.* T. & T. Clark Study Guides. Edinburgh: T. & T. Clark, 1995.

Barton, John. "The Prophets and the Cult." In *Temple and Worship in Biblical Israel,* edited by John Day, 111–22. Library of Hebrew Bible/Old Testament Studies 422. New York: T. & T. Clark, 2005.

Berquist, Jon L. "Dangerous Waters of Justice and Righteousness: Amos 5:18–27." *BTB* 23 (1993) 54–63.

Beuken, Willem A. M. *Jesaja 1–12.* HKAT. Freiburg: Herder, 2003.

Bič, Milos. "Der Prophet Amos—ein Haepatoskopos." *VT* 1 (1951) 293–96.

Blenkinsopp, Joseph. *Isaiah 1–39.* AB 19. New York: Doubleday, 2000.

Bloch-Smith, Elizabeth. *Judahite Burial Practices and Beliefs about the Dead.* JSOTSup 123. ASOR Monograph Series 7. Sheffield: Sheffield Academic, 1992.

Boecker, Hans Jochen. *Law and the Administration of Justice in the Old Testament and Ancient East.* Translated by Jeremy Moiser. Minneapolis: Augsburg, 1980.

———. "Überlegungen zur Kultpolemik der vorexilischen Propheten." In *Die Botschaft und die Boten: Festschrift für Hans Walter Wolff zum 70. Geburtstag*, edited by Jörg Jeremias and Lothar Perlitt, 169–80. Neukirchen-Vluyn: Neukirchener, 1981.

Boer, Pieter Arie Hendrik de. "An Aspect of Sacrifice." In *Studies in the Religion of Ancient Israel*, edited by Helmer Ringgren et. al., 27–47. VTSup 23. Leiden: Brill, 1972.

Borowski, Oded. *Daily Life in Biblical Times*. Archaeology and Biblical Studies 5. Atlanta: Society of Biblical Literature, 2003.

Brettler, Marc Zvi. "Nevi'im." In *The Jewish Study Bible*. Edited by Adele Berlin and Marc Zvi Brettler. New York: Oxford University Press, 2004.

Brueggemann, Walter. *Theology of the Old Testament: Testimony, Dispute, Advocacy*. Minneapolis: Fortress, 1997.

———. *Isaiah 1–39*. Westminster Bible Companion. Louisville: Westminster John Knox, 1998.

Burkert, Walter. *Homo Necans: The Anthropology of Ancient Greek Sacrificial Ritual and Myth*. Translated by Peter Bing. Berkeley: University of California Press, 1983.

Childs, Brevard S. *Isaiah*. OTL. Louisville: Westminster John Knox, 2001.

Chinitz, Jacob. "Were the Prophets Opposed to Sacrifice?" *Jewish Biblical Quarterly* 36 (2008) 73–80.

Clements, Ronald E. and H.-J. Fabry, "מַיִם, *mayim*." In *TDOT* 8:265–88.

Cripps, Richard S. *A Commentary on the Book of Amos*. 2nd ed. Limited Classical Reprint Library. Minneapolis: Klock & Klock, 1981.

Driggers, I. Brent. "Israel in God's Country: Amos 5:21–24 in Context." *Koinonia* 9:1–2 (1997) 20–36.

Duhm, Bernhard. *Das Buch Jesaja*. HKAT 3. Göttingen: Vandenhoeck & Ruprecht, 1892 (4th ed. 1922).

Eakin, Frank E. Jr. *The Religion and Culture of Israel: An Introduction to Old Testament Thought*. Boston: Allyn & Bacon, 1971.

Ernst, Alexander B. *Weisheitliche Kultkritik: Zu Theologie und Ethik des Sprüchebuchs und der Prophetie des 8. Jahrhunderts*. BibS(N) 23. Neukirchen-Vluyn: Neukirchener, 1994.

Fabry, Heinz-Josef, and Moshe Weinfeld. "מִנְחָה, *minḥâ*." In *TDOT* 8:407–21.

Falk, Ze'ev W. "Law and Ethics in the Hebrew Bible." In *Justice and Righteousness: Biblical Themes and Their Influence*, edited by Henning Graf Reventlow and Yair Hoffman, 82–90. JSOTSup 137. Sheffield: JSOT Press, 1992.

Farr, Georges. "The Language of Amos, Popular or Cultic?" *VT* 16 (1966) 312–24.

Fey, Reinhard. *Amos und Jesaja: Abhängigkeit und Eigenständigkeit des Jesaja*. WMANT 12. Neukirchen-Vluyn: Neukirchener, 1963.

Fitzmyer, Joseph A. *Responses to 101 Questions on the Dead Sea Scrolls*. New York: Paulist, 1992.

Frey, Christofer. "The Impact of the Biblical Idea of Justice on Present Discussions of Social Justice." In *Justice and Righteousness: Biblical Themes and Their Influence*, edited by Henning Graf Reventlow and Yair Hoffman, 91–104. JSOTSup 137. Sheffield: JSOT Press, 1992.

Geus, C. H. J. de. *Towns in Ancient Israel and in the Southern Levant*. Palaestina Antiqua 10. Leuven: Peeters, 2003.

Girard, René. *Violence and the Sacred*. Translated by Patrick Gregory. Baltimore: Johns Hopkins University Press, 1977.

Gray, George Buchanan. *A Critical and Exegetical Commentary on the Book of Isaiah I–XXXIX.* 2 vols. ICC. New York: Scribner, 1912.

———. *Sacrifice in the Old Testament: Its Theory and Practice.* Edited by Harry M. Orlinsky. 1925. Reprinted, Library of Biblical Studies. New York: Ktav, 1971.

Haran, Menahem. *Temples and Temple-Service in Ancient Israel: An Inquiry into the Character of Cult Phenomena and the Historical Setting of the Priestly School.* 1978. Reprinted, Winona Lake, IN: Eisenbrauns, 1985.

Havice, Harriet. "The Concern for the Widow and the Fatherless in the Ancient Near East." Ph.D. diss. Yale University, 1979.

Hertzberg, Hans Wilhelm. *Beiträge zur Traditionsgeschichte und Theologie des Alten Testaments.* Göttingen: Vandenhoeck & Ruprecht, 1962.

Hoffmeier, James K. "Egypt's Role in the Events of 701 B.C.: A Rejoinder to J. J. M. Roberts." In *Jerusalem in Bible and Archaeology: The First Temple Period,* edited by Andrew G. Vaughn and Ann E. Killebrew, 285–89. Leiden: Brill, 2003.

Houston, Walter. "Was There a Social Crisis in the Eighth Century?" In *In Search of Pre-exilic Israel: Proceedings of the Oxford Old Testament Seminar,* edited by John Day, 130–49. London: T. & T. Clark, 2004.

Hyman, Ronald T. "Amos 5:24 Prophetic, Chastising, Surprising, Poetic." *Jewish Bible Quarterly* 30 (2002) 227–34.

Irvine, Stuart A. *Isaiah, Ahaz, and the Syro-Ephraimitic Crisis.* SBLDS 123. Atlanta: Scholars, 1989.

Jensen, Joseph. *The Use of tôrâ by Isaiah: His Debate with the Wisdom Tradition.* CBQMS 3. Washington, DC: Catholic Biblical Association, 1973.

———. *Isaiah 1–39.* OTM 8. Wilmington, DE: Glazier, 1984.

———. *Ethical Dimensions of the Prophets.* Collegeville, MN: Liturgical, 2006.

Jeremias, Jörg. *The Book of Amos: A Commentary.* Translated by Douglas W. Stott. OTL. Louisville: Westminster John Knox, 1995.

Joüon, Paul. *A Grammar of Biblical Hebrew: Part Three: Syntax: Paradigms and Indices.* Translated and revised by T. Muraoka. 2 vols. Subsidia Biblica 14/1–2. Rome: Pontifical Biblical Institute, 1991.

Kaiser, Otto. *Isaiah 1–12: A Commentary.* Translated by John Bowden. 2nd ed. OTL. Philadelphia: Westminster, 1983.

———. "Kult und Kultkritik im Alten Testament." In *"Und Mose schrieb dieses Lied auf": Studien zum Alten Testament und zum Alten Orient: Festschrift für Oswald Loretz zur Vollendung seines 70. Lebensjahres mit Beiträgen von Freunden, Schülern und Kollegen,* edited by Manfried Dietrich and Ingo Kottsieper, 401–26. AOAT 250. Münster: Ugarit-Verlag, 1998.

Kellermann, D. "עוֹלָה/עֹלָה, 'ōlâ/'ōlâ." In *TDOT* 11:96–113.

King, Philip J. *Amos, Hosea, Micah—An Archaeological Commentary.* Philadelphia: Westminster, 1988.

King, Philip J., and Lawrence E. Stager. *Life in Biblical Israel.* Library of Ancient Israel. Louisville: Westminster John Knox, 2001.

Klawans, Jonathan. *Purity, Sacrifice, and the Temple: Symbolism and Supercessionism in the Study of Ancient Judaism.* New York: Oxford University Press, 2006.

Koch, K. "מוֹעֵד, môʿēd." In *TDOT* 8:167–73.

Kornfeld, Walter. "Die Gesellschafts- und Kultkritik alttestamentlicher Propheten." In *Leiturgia, Koinonia, Diakonia: Festschrift für Kardinal Franz König zum 75. Geburtstag,* edited by Raphael Schulte, 181–200. Vienna: Herder, 1980.

Kugel, James L. *The Idea of Biblical Poetry: Parallelism and Its History*. Baltimore: Johns Hopkins University Press, 1981.

Lipinski, Edward. "שְׂנֵא, *śānē'*; שׂנֵא, *śōnē'*; מִשְׂנֶא, *mᵉśānē'*; שִׂנְאָה, *śinâ*." In *TDOT* 14:164–74.

Loretz, Oswald. "Die babylonischen Gottesnamen Sukkut und Kajjamānu in Amos 5,26: Ein Beitrag zur jüdischen Astrologie." *ZAW* 101 (1989) 286–89.

Lucas, Ernest C. "Sacrifice in the Prophets." In *Sacrifice in the Bible*, edited by Roger T. Beckwith and Martin J. Selma, 59–74. Grand Rapids: Baker, 1995.

Marti, Karl. *Das Dodekapropheten eklärt*. KAT 13. Tübingen: Mohr/Siebeck, 1904.

Martínez, Florentino García, and Eibert J. C. Tigchelaar. *The Dead Sea Scrolls Study Edition*. 2 vols. Leiden: Brill, 1997.

Mays, James Luther. *Amos: A Commentary*. OTL. Philadelphia: Westminster, 1969.

Meyers, Carol. "Temple, Jerusalem." In *ABD* 6:351–69.

Milgrom, Jacob. *Studies in Cultic Theology and Terminology*. SJLA 36. Leiden: Brill, 1983.

Motyer, J. Alec. *The Prophecy of Isaiah: An Introduction and Commentary*. Downers Grove, IL: InterVarsity, 1993.

Nel, Philip J. "Social Justice as Religious Responsibility in Near Eastern Religions: Historic Ideal and Ideological Illusion." *JNSL* 26 (2000) 143–53.

Netzer, Ehud. "Domestic Architecture in the Iron Age." In *The Architecture of Ancient Israel: From the Prehistoric to the Persian Periods*, edited by Aharon Kempinski and Ronny Reich, 193–201. Israel Exploration Society. Jerusalem: Ahva, 1992.

Oswalt, John N. *The Book of Isaiah: Chapters 1–39*. NICOT. Grand Rapids: Eerdmans, 1986.

Parry, Donald W., and Elisha Qimron, editors. *The Great Isaiah Scroll (1QIsaᵃ): A New Edition*. STDJ 32. Boston: Brill, 1999.

Paul, Shalom M. *Amos: A Commentary on the Book of Amos*. Hermeneia. Minneapolis: Fortress, 1991.

Pfeiffer, Robert H. *Introduction to the Old Testament*. New York: Harper, 1951.

———, translator. "Counsels of Wisdom." In *ANET*, 426–27.

Premnath, Devadasan N. *Eighth Century Prophets: A Social Analysis*. St. Louis: Chalice, 2003.

Roberts, J. J. M. "In Defense of the Monarchy: The Contribution of Israelite Kingship to Biblical Theology." In *Ancient Israelite Religion: Essays in Honor of Frank Moore Cross*, edited by Patrick D. Miller et al., 377–96. Philadelphia: Fortress, 1987.

———. "Egypt, Assyria, Isaiah, and the Ashdod Affair: An Alternative Proposal." In *Jerusalem in Bible and Archaeology: The First Temple Period*, edited by Andrew G. Vaughn and Ann E. Killebrew, 265–83. Leiden: Brill, 2003.

Robinson, Theodore H. *Prophecy and the Prophets in Ancient Israel*. 2nd ed. London: Duckworth, 1953.

Rotzell, Dirk U. *Studien zur Redaktion und Komposition des Amosbuches*. BZAW 243. Berlin: de Gruyter, 1996.

Rowley, Harold H. *From Moses to Qumran: Studies in the Old Testament*. New York: Association, 1963.

Seitz, Christopher R. *Isaiah 1–39*. Interpretation. Louisville: John Knox, 1993.

Smith, Mark S. *The Early History of God: Yahweh and the Other Deities in Ancient Israel*. 2nd ed. Biblical Resource Series. Grand Rapids: Eerdmans, 2002.

Snijders, L. A. "נָחַל, *naḥal*; אֵיתָן, *'êṭān*." In *TDOT* 9:335–40.

Snijders, L. A., Helmer Ringgren, and Heinz-Josef Fabry. "נָהָר, *nāhār*; נָהָר, *nāhar*." In *TDOT* 9:261–70.

Soggin, J. Alberto. *The Prophet Amos: A Translation and Commentary.* Translated by John Bowden. London: SCM, 1987.

Sweeney, Marvin A. *Isaiah 1–39: With an Introduction to Prophetic Literature.* FOTL 16. Grand Rapids: Eerdmans, 1996.

Ussishkin, David. "Sennacherib's Campaign to Philistia and Judah: Ekron, Lachish, and Jerusalem." In *Essays on Ancient Israel in Its Near Eastern Context: A Tribute to Nadav Na'aman,* edited by Yairah Amit et al., 339–57. Winona Lake, IN: Eisenbrauns, 2006.

Vaux, Roland de. *Ancient Israel: Its Life and Institutions.* Translated by John McHugh. 1961. Reprinted, Biblical Resource Series 3. Grand Rapids: Eerdmans, 1997.

Waltke, Bruce K., and Michael P. O'Connor. *An Introduction to Biblical Hebrew Syntax.* Winona Lake, IN: Eisenbrauns, 1990.

Watts, John D. W. *Vision and Prophecy in Amos.* Expanded Anniversary ed. Macon, GA: Mercer University Press, 1997.

Weinfeld, Moshe. "'Justice and Righteousness'—וצדקה משפט—The Expression and Its Meaning." In *Justice and Righteousness: Biblical Themes and Their Influence,* edited by Henning Graf Reventlow and Yair Hoffman, 228–46. JSOTSup 137. Sheffield: Sheffield University Press, 1992.

———. *Social Justice in Ancient Israel and in the Ancient Near East.* Minneapolis: Fortress, 1995.

Weiss, Meir. "Concerning Amos' Repudiation of the Cult." In *Pomegranates and Golden Bells: Studies in Biblical, Jewish, and Near Eastern Ritual, Law, and Literature in Honor of Jacob Milgrom,* edited by David P. Wright et al., 199–214. Winona Lake, IN: Eisenbrauns, 1995.

Wellhausen, Julius. *Prolegomena to the History of Ancient Israel:* With a reprint of the article "Israel" from the Encyclopaedia Britannica. 1957. Reprinted, Eugene, OR: Wipf and Stock, 2003.

Westermann, Claus. *Elements of Old Testament Theology.* Translated by Douglas W. Stott. Atlanta: John Knox, 1982.

Whitley, Charles Francis. *The Prophetic Achievement.* London: Mowbray, 1963.

Wildberger, Hans. *Isaiah 1–12: A Commentary.* Translated by Thomas H. Trapp. Continental Commentaries. Minneapolis: Fortress, 1991.

———. *Isaiah 13–27.* Translated by Thomas H. Trapp. Continental Commentaries. Minneapolis: Fortress, 1997.

———. *Isaiah 28–39.* Translated by Thomas H. Trapp. Continental Commentaries. Minneapolis: Fortress, 2002.

Wolfe, Rolland. *Meet Amos and Hosea: the Prophets of Israel.* New York: Harper & Brothers, 1945.

Wolff, Hans Walter. *Joel and Amos.* Translated by Waldemar Janzen, S. Dean McBride Jr., and Charles A. Muenchow. Hermeneia. Philadelphia: Fortress, 1977.

Yadin, Yigael. *Hazor: The Rediscovery of a Great Citadel of the Bible.* New York: Random House, 1975.

Younger, K. Lawson. "Assyrian Involvement in the Southern Levant at the End of the Eighth Century B.C.E." In *Jerusalem in Bible and Archaeology: The First Temple Period,* edited by Andrew G. Vaughn and Ann E. Killebrew, 235–63. Leiden: Brill, 2003.